MW00781000

Wherever I Go, I Will
Always Be a Loyal American

Wherever I Go, I Will Always Be a Loyal American

Schooling Seattle's Japanese Americans
during World War II

★ ★ ★ ★ ★

YOON K. PAK

RoutledgeFalmer
New York & London

Published in 2002 by
RoutledgeFalmer
29 West 35th Street
New York, NY 10001

Published in Great Britain by
RoutledgeFalmer
11 New Fetter Lane
London EC4P 4EE

RoutledgeFalmer is an imprint of the Taylor & Francis Group.

Printed in the United States of America on acid-free paper.

Portions of this book have been previously published in *Theory and Research in Social Education,* Vol. 28, No/ 3 (Summer 2000): 339–358. © College and University Faculty Assembly of National Council for the Social Studies.

10   9   8   7   6   5   4   3   2   1

Cataloging-in-Publication Data

Pak, Yoon K.
    Wherever I go I will always be a loyal American : schooling Seattle's Japanese Americans during World War II / Yoon K. Pak.
        p. cm—(Studies in the history of education ; v. 13)
    Includes bibliographical references and index.
    ISBN 0-415-93234-3—ISBN 0-415-93235-1 (pbk.)
        1. Japanese-Americans—Education—Washington (State)—Seattle. 2. World War, 1939-1945—Japanese Americans—Education (Primary)—Washington (State)—Seattle. 3. World War, 1939-1945—Washington (State)—Seattle. I. Title. II. Studies in the history of education (RoutledgeFalmer (Firm)) ; . 13.

LC3175.S43 P35 2001
371.829'95'60797772—dc21   2001019963

FOR MY GRANDMOTHER
WHO TAUGHT ME THE VALUE OF STORIES

CONTENTS

★ ★ ★ ★ ★

PREFACE

★ ★ ★ ★ ★

This book was an accident waiting to happen.

My former doctoral adviser at the University of Washington, Professor Nancy Beadie, assigned me, as part of requisite coursework, to conduct archival research at the university's Manuscripts and Archives Division on an area related to educational history. Having grown up in Tacoma, Washington, I proceeded to investigate a teacher who had taught in the working-class industrial town once touted as the "city of destiny" during the peak of the Alaskan gold rush. I carefully recorded the accession number for the teacher's files and waited eagerly for the archivist to return. What I received was not what I had requested. I double-checked the accession number against the original on the request form and found that I had transposed numbers—something that, as those who know me are aware, I tend to do regularly, usually resulting in dire consequences. Needless to say, it worked in my favor this time around.

I opened the thick, red notebook binder, meticulously organized and ready for a researcher's perusal, and started reading:

March 29, 1942
Dear Miss Evanson,
    We are leaving our city, to where I am going I am wholly ignorant. However I am not unhappy, nor do I have objections for as long as this evacuation is for the benefit of the United State. But I do am regreting about leaving this school and the thought that I shall not see for a long while pains me extremely. Your pleasant ways of teaching had made my heart yearn for the days when I was in your

classroom. Your kind smile and your wonderful work you did for me shall be one of my pleasant memories.

Tooru

March 24, [19]42

Dear Miss Evanson,

Because of this situation, we are asked to leave this dear city of Seattle and its surroundings. I am sure I will miss my teachers and Mr. Sears. There was never a school like Washington School and I sure will miss it. As for me, the one I will miss the most will be you. You have been very patient and kind throughout my work. If the school I will attend next would have a teacher like you I will be only too glad. When I am on my way my memories will flow back to the time I was attending this school and the assemblies that were held in the hall.

Wherever I go I will be a loyal American.

Love,

Emiko

Another small set of letters written only two months later came from a detention camp in Puyallup, Washington. The students' new home was a horse stall in a fairground, where they had to make their own mattresses and pillows out of straw hay. According to some students, their lives had become regimented, controlled by a bugle's reveille. These students' temporary lives in "Camp Harmony" were a prelude to their permanent incarceration in Minidoka, Idaho, and Tule Lake, California:

Puyallup Assembly Center

D-1-22

Puyallup, Wash.

Dear Miss Evanson,

How are you and are you having a good time? I am but I'm getting quite lonesome because I am missing my studies. Although there isn't any school over here I use some of the studies I was taught by you and now am I glad. Since I came here the only thing you could do at home is to study and write letters so when I begin writing letters I take all the steps I learned.

Now I will be closing for I will have to write to the 7B3's so Good
bye and Good Luck
A pupil, Yeoko

B-2-48 Camp Harmony
Puyallup, Wash.
May 10, 1942
Dear Miss Evanson,
    How are you? I am fine, but I had my Typhoid shot and now I have
a headache, and my arm aches.
    I arrived in Puyallup, Friday. We passed Kent, Auburn, Sumner,
and then to our camp. I guess your wondering why we came here so
late. Well, we were delayed because we had to go to the Clinic.
    We have to make our own chairs, and tables, and the mattress for
the bed with hay in it. (Isn't it terrible.)
    How is the class? Are there any Japanese in the class (7B3) like
Yeoko? If she is there would you ask her for her address?
    We eat from 6 to 7 (morning) 11:30 to 2:30 (afternoon) 5 to 6
o'clock in the evening.
    The shacks are cold and has holes in between the logs. Our place
is in Camp B.
Your friend, Mary
    P.S. Please write to me, and the class also because it is lonely
here. May I have your picture too?

Consumed by emotions, I began to imagine how difficult their lives must have been at that historical moment as they grappled with the dissonance of democratic equality and race discrimination. My previous reading and courses I had taken in Asian American studies helped to provide intellectual and theoretical groundwork for how and why the imprisonment of Japanese Americans occurred, but I wasn't prepared to be personally transformed by the content of what these children wrote.

It was almost as if fate had *wanted* me to transpose those numbers. The Ella Evanson Papers, accession number 2402 (which I have now memorized!), include, among other items, letters, essays, and farewell entries by Japanese American students contemplating their forced removal from their homes during World War II. Ella Evanson wanted, or better yet needed, someone to work with her collection. I heeded her call.

Over the course of working with these sets of letters, I could see the students' emphasis on what the schools were attempting to teach about democratic citizenship education. Tolerance, equality, and racial understanding emerged from the students' compositions time and again. This made me curious to know how the schools had reacted to the incarceration order, and I wanted to trace the tradition of their seemingly progressive pedagogy. In investigating the history of the Seattle public schools in the 1940s, I looked to school policies ranging from Americanization to citizenship and character education from the 1910s to the 1940s. In this book I explore the contradiction between the schools' mission to educate for democracy and the forced incarceration, foregrounded by the letters and essays written by students at the very moment the historical events took place.

ACKNOWLEDGMENTS

★ ★ ★ ★ ★

In the course of researching and writing this book I have received much support, of which I was undeserving, for I have taken more than I could possibly ever give. Key individuals at the University of Washington deserve high praise for their pursuit of excellence and support for minority graduate students. A tremendous gratitude is owed to Nancy Beadie who, as my doctoral adviser, provided me with the opportunity to pursue my interest in history and Asian American studies. Her patience and guidance are values I hope to emulate to my students. Nancy has read more portions of this manuscript than I care to mention and has provided critical commentary throughout all phases of the revision process. I take full responsibility, however, for any errors that may occur. I wish to thank Donna Kerr for helping me, and a new generation of scholars, to consider the human face of education. Deborah Kerdeman and Edward Taylor are also among those rare individuals who combine intellectualism with compassion. Tetsuden Kashima helped me to understand the complex histories of Japanese Americans and to see the incarceration as an issue central to democracy. Walter Parker's courses on democratic citizenship provided me with the framework to situate the students' writings.

Throughout my undergraduate and graduate years at UW, the Graduate School's Fellowship and Assistantship Division and the Minority Education Division have provided me with financial support above and beyond their call of duty. Nola Blanes, former division head of Fellowships and Assistantships, and Cynthia Morales, assistant to the dean, have dedicated much of their professional and personal lives to student services in higher education.

One cannot downplay the importance of archivists and librarians in conducting historical research. I am grateful for the assistance of Eleanor Toews, archivist for the Seattle Public Schools Archives and Records Management Center and Karyl Winn, Curator of Manuscripts at the University of Washington's libraries. Their thoughtfulness and consideration in providing me with leads to sources I had not considered made my work more fulfilling.

The College of Education and the Educational Policy Studies Department at the University of Illinois at Urbana-Champaign have provided research funds and the time required to complete this manuscript. My colleague and department head James Anderson has been a continuing source of support.

The editors and reviewers at RoutledgeFalmer have made the manuscript writing experience a pleasure, and I owe them thanks.

Without the mentoring of Ron Rochon, and his sustained support and friendship, my career in academe would not have been possible. The Washington State University's 1997 summer doctoral fellowship, under his direction, proved an invaluable experience. My fellow twelve women ("fellas") of the program, who are now doctors, will always have a special place in my heart.

Without the assistance of Shirley Shimada and Mako Nakagawa, my interviews with Hisako Kato, Mitsie Fujii, and Kazuo Ishimitsu would not have been possible. This book is more complete because of all their willingness to share a piece of themselves with me.

Matthew Walch has been a grounding force and best friend for most of my life. I am most fortunate to have his love, patience, and understanding.

Finally, I wish to give thanks to my parents, Un Sik and Kwang Suk Pak, my aunts and uncles George T. and Kwang Soon Guy, and Reverend Kyung Joo and Jong Ja Kim, my sister Frances Pak, and my brother and his family Jacob, Rachel, Justine, and Kristyan Pak. Though we were not blessed with financial riches as an immigrant family from Korea, the sustenance of their prayers (and food) have provided me with spiritual wealth beyond imagination.

DEFINITION OF TERMS

★ ★ ★ ★ ★

Issei (ee-say): First-generation immigrant Japanese

Nisei (nee-say): Second-generation Japanese Americans (U.S. citizens)

Nikkei (nee-kay): Those of Japanese ancestry

Nihonmachi: Japantown

INTRODUCTION

★ ★ ★ ★ ★

Lives are not stories. A day, a month, a year, or a lifetime has no plot. Our experiences are only the raw stuff of stories. The beginnings of our lives are arbitrary; usually their endings come too soon or too late for any neat narrative conclusions.

—Richard White, *Remembering Ahanagran: Storytelling in a Family's Past*

In documenting the life of his mother, the historian Richard White recounts the tension between the disparate experiences of a lived life and the task of the historian to draw out a cohesive story based upon the lives of historical subjects. In a sense, that has been one of the major challenges in depicting the lives of Seattle's Japanese American schoolchildren on the eve of their incarceration. The story of the incarceration itself does not represent the sole experience of Japanese Americans in the United States: they have led complex lives marked by policies of racial discrimination in our past. But to depict *only* a history of victimization shortchanges the depth of their experiences in which they have played an active role for themselves and for their offspring. I have been fortunate to draw upon the growing historical scholarship on and about Japanese Americans' experiences[1] to lend context in my attempt to draw a narrative—marked more by clutter than neatness.

In viewing history as stories of everyday people, living everyday lives, disrupted by ephemeral moments testing the bounds of humanity, I highlight the experiences of students during a time of war. The students of Washington School, by providing their thoughts in writing, help us to shape a deeper understanding and interpretation of the events on the eve of the incarceration. The actions of the government, albeit an important factor in deciding historical events, are better understood in the context of the participants for whom the exclusionary policies were effected.

To be sure, living with the dissonance between the democratic ideal of equality and structural racial discrimination has been a normative and stultifying experience for Asian Americans in the United States. The desire to belong with the reality of not quite belonging was, and is, a recurring theme of Asian Americans' relegation to the margins of society. The Filipino American intellectual Carlos Bulosan, in *America Is in the Heart,* marveled at the paradox of America, in its capacity to show love and hate: "Why was America so kind and yet so cruel? Was there no way to simplifying [*sic*] things in this continent so that suffering would be minimized? Was there no common denominator on which we could all meet? I was angry and confused, and wondered if I would ever understand this paradox."[2] Bulosan's perceptive observation, coupled with the painful reality in which he lived the paradox, provides a useful lens in examining the lives of Seattle's Nisei youth on the eve of their incarceration. They were equal yet not quite equal. Schoolteachers and administrators emphasized all along the message of tolerance and equality among different ethnic groups, in viewing everyone as an American. The government, on the other hand, viewed Japanese residents and citizens with suspicion. Contrasting messages of what it meant to live in a democracy during wartime became embodied in the lives of these youth.

While perhaps the Nisei students in my study were unaware of their complex subjectivities rooted in the history of Japanese America, they captured the essence of the discordant view through their proclamation of loyalty to the United States. The fact that many pronounced their American identity meant that that very identity was held suspect. Indeed, the meaning of citizenship for Nisei was called into question by the forced imprisonment[3] of Japanese American and permanent residents on the West Coast of the United States with the signing of Executive Order 9066 by President Franklin D. Roosevelt on February 19, 1942. Despite the lessons of citizenship the Seattle schools were trying to teach their students, the reality of

Nisei as citizens turned out to be far different from the principle. Writing to their teacher in response to the executive order, the students were attempting to make sense of the dissonance between the idea of citizenship on the one hand, and the experience of being treated as an "enemy alien," on the other.

HOMEROOM TEACHER, ELLA EVANSON, AND HER STUDENTS

The students' compositions were the personal collection of their homeroom teacher, Ella Evanson, of Washington School. Evanson taught seventh and eighth grade English and social studies and was later the school's librarian. A *Seattle Times Magazine* article on Evanson provides a short account of her teaching career.[4] Evanson was a native of North Dakota and taught there for a few years. After working for the government in Washington, D.C., during World War I, she came to Seattle and earned a Washington State teaching certificate at Bellingham. She taught for a year in Everett, commuting daily on the interurban. She then taught at B. F. Day Elementary School in Seattle before going to Washington School in 1928. She was there until her retirement in 1956. By then, Washington was a junior high school. She spoke fondly of the principal, Mr. Sears, and how he stressed the importance of America as a country of many different cultures and races. After her retirement, Evanson went on a freighter trip across the Pacific and continued traveling around the world for more than a year. She traveled extensively for several years and forgot about the collection of letters, until she happened upon them some time later. She died in January 1986 at the age of eighty-eight.[5]

At the time of the newspaper interview in 1974[6] Evanson, a septuagenarian, was quoted as saying that the letters showed a general acceptance of the evacuation as justified, even though the Japanese American children regretted having to leave and their schoolmates were sorry to see them go. "I remember how difficult it was when the children had to say good-bye to their friends and board buses for the relocation center at Puyallup. . . . Many

3

of the Japanese-American children took their pets and gave them to their friends because they weren't allowed to keep them. It was a very emotional experience. Many of the children were weeping."[7]

The students' writings might reveal such sentiments on the surface, but a critical examination into the nature of what students wrote, in the context of the political situation of the time, reveals another story that Evanson might have neglected to recall at the time of her interview. The popular presses in the 1940s did indicate a "general acceptance" by Nikkei of the incarceration orders. However, the public acts amid private fears were hardly congruent. On the one hand, Nikkei's public act of loyalty toward the United States stemmed in part from their efforts to "do what the government ordered." On the other hand, the private reactions and fears prompted by Executive Order 9066 were always there.[8] This book problematizes the idea of "general acceptance" on the part of Japanese Americans by going beyond the surface of the students' writings and the response by Evanson herself. Very few choices existed for Nikkei when Executive Order 9066 was signed. Older Nisei who publicly resisted governmental orders were arrested and imprisoned. The "general acceptance" on the part of Japanese Americans was due to the fact that very little could be done about the impending imprisonment. The public, on the other hand, typically viewed "general acceptance" as indicating Nikkei's volunteerism and obeisance to governmental orders of evacuation "for their own good." The multiple layers of meaning embedded in the students' simple phrases are beset with issues of identity and citizenship, and how they fit within the context of democracy.

This book comprises four sets of writings. The first set comes from an English class writing assignment in which students reflected on their school's assembly performed the day after the bombing of Pearl Harbor. The message of tolerance by the principal, Arthur G. Sears, is resoundingly clear as expressed by the students. The second set contains farewell entries by Nisei in a journal made for Ella Evanson by one of her students. While a districtwide request went out to gather writings by Nisei on the eve of their incarceration, it is not possible to ascertain whether the farewell entries were a part of this project. It is more likely that the students were writing for Evanson only. The third collection is non-Nisei reflections on the "evacuation." They write about how the evacuation of their Nisei classmates would affect their friendships and relationships. The final set of writings, interspersed throughout the book, comes from Nisei at a detention center in Puyallup, Washington, ironically called "Camp Harmony." The letters to Evanson reveal the drudgery of life without school and their former classmates, as well as the necessity of adjusting to a regimented life signaled by bugle calls. Taken in their entirety the students' writings provide perspectives on what Washington School was doing to address wartime events and how the students internalized school policies of tolerance, given the national message of race hatred against the Japanese. The letters signify and incorporate the totality of the students' lived realities in the short but expressive phrases. Ideas of loyalty, democracy, citizenship, the threat of possible violence, and how school officials were helping to cope are unveiled. The most expressive ideas disclose feelings of uncertainty at what the future will hold and of the sadness of Nisei students having to leave their home. The uprooting of one's birthplace, as also expressed in the narrator's accounts, to a place unknown created extreme anxieties, to say the least. Proof of one's loyalty and American identity became a focal point for many Nisei as they were preparing to leave Seattle. Perhaps the opportunity to express the chaotic experiences of being uprooted provided a vehicle for students to attempt to make sense of dissonance.

CHAPTER OUTLINES

In writing this book I made a conscious decision not to provide a more general history of Seattle or of Japanese Americans in the United States, both topics worthy of historical investigation. I feel that my more focused and unique approach to sharing the voices of students through their writings, couched within a democratic citizenship framework, places them at the center of my study, a goal I wanted to achieve early on. This method appealed to me in that the history of education is replete with administrative and policy studies affecting schooling but has seen very few tending to concentrate on classroom culture and the lives of students. The writings by middle school students in 1941–1942 offer primary source evidence that weighs equally with official school documents in the history of education. What students say, and how they say it, matters.

To achieve my goal I have organized this book around particular themes rather than as a chronological account of the events surrounding schooling and World War II. Chapter 1 lays the foundation of the book as I present the attempts by Japanese American and non–Japanese American students to make sense of dissonance upon hearing the news of the Executive Order 9066. This foregrounding of letters makes for better understanding of the subsequent chapters.

Chapter 2 examines the early history of Seattle, paying particular attention to immigration restrictions and anti-Japanese activities along the West Coast of the United States. The early educational histories of Seattle's Nisei, including the influence of the Japanese Language Schools, are discussed.

Chapter 3 looks back at the tradition of Americanization and citizenship in the Seattle schools from 1916 up to the 1930s in which loyalty and patriotism were the overarching ideals that the Seattle Schools sought to inculcate in the young. Various curricular and extracurricular reforms to improve citizenship and moral character, alongside a comparative framework of programs nationwide, are included.

Chapter 4 is an extension of the schools' lessons on citizenship in the 1930s. I pay particular attention to the ideals of tolerance and interculturalism as influenced by national educational organizations such as the Progressive Education Association and the National Education Association. Locally, two curriculum guides, *Successful Living* and *Living Today— Learning for Tomorrow*, are the primary sources Seattle schoolteachers and administrators used in implementing character and moral education—a natural extension of American and citizenship education.

Chapter 5 combines the schools' tradition of democratic citizenship with the community's response to war. Schools oftentimes act as a mirror to the events that unfold in the local communities. Tensions and conflicts that plague communities also work their way into schools. Likewise the growing prejudice that evolved in Seattle against Nikkei, which was further exacerbated by the media, seeped into the minds of Seattle's schoolchildren. The letters of Washington's students make reference to conflicts and tensions developing in their communities.

Chapter 6 focuses on three Nisei who attended Washington School on the eve of their incarceration. Their oral histories touch on their lives and identities in schools and outside the schools, and how that was jarred by the news of being forced to leave their homes. Their individual stories shed light on how contingent their identities as Nisei were. The oral histories provide a more complex and rich narrative that sometimes works against the grain of popular knowledge on Nisei identity development. Included in the chapter is a further exploration of how the oral history narrators analyzed the themes in the students' letters that were not only making sense of dissonance but embodied dissonance.

EXECUTIVE ORDER NO. 9066

Whereas, the successful prosecution of the war requires every possible protection against espionage and against sabotage to national-defense material, national-defense premises and national-defense utilities as defined in Section 4, Act of April 20, 1918, 40 x Stat. 533, as amended by the Act of November 30, 1940, 54 Stat. 1220, and the Act of August 21, 1941, 55 Stat. 655 (U.S.C., Title 50, Sec. 104):

Now therefore, by virtue of the authority vested in me as President of the United States, and Commander in Chief of the Army and Navy, I hereby authorize and direct the Secretary of War, and the Military Commanders whom he may from time to time designate, whenever he or any designated Commander deems such action necessary or desirable, to prescribe military areas in such places and of such extent as he or the appropriate Military Commander may determine, from which any or all persons may be excluded, and with respect to which, the right of any person to enter, remain in, or leave shall be subject to whatever restriction the Secretary of

War or the appropriate Military Commander may impose in his discretion. The Secretary of War is hereby authorized to provide food, shelter, and other accommodations as may be necessary, in the judgment of the Secretary of War or the said Military Commander, and until other arrangements are made, to accomplish the purpose of this order. The designation of military areas in any region or locality shall supersede designations of prohibited and restricted areas by the Proclamation of December 7 and 8, 1941, and shall supersede the responsibility and authority of the Attorney General under the said Proclamations in respect of such prohibited and restricted areas.

I hereby further authorize and direct the Secretary of War and the said Military Commanders to take such other steps as he or the appropriate Military Commander may deem advisable to enforce compliance with the restrictions applicable to each Military area herein above authorized to be designated, including the use of Federal troops and other Federal Agencies, with authority to accept assistance of state and local agencies.

I hereby further authorize and direct all Executive Departments, independent establishments and other Federal Agencies, to assist the Secretary of War or the said Military Commanders in carrying out this Executive Order, including the furnishing of medical aid, hospitalization, food, clothing, transportation, use of land, shelter, and other supplies, equipment, utilities, facilities, and services.

This order shall not be construed as modifying or limiting in any way the authority heretofore granted under Executive Order No. 8972, dated December 12, 1941, nor shall it be construed as limiting or modifying the duty and responsibility of the Federal Bureau of Investigation, with respect to the investigations of alleged acts of sabotage or the duty and responsibility of the Attorney General and the Department of Justice under the Proclamations of December 7 and 8, 1941, prescribing regulations for the conduct and control of alien enemies, except as such duty and responsibility is superseded by the designation of military areas hereunder.

The White House, February 19, 1942   Franklin D. Roosevelt.

Chapter 1

MAKING SENSE OF DISSONANCE:

STUDENTS' RESPONSE

TO EXECUTIVE ORDER 9066

★　★　★　★　★

President Roosevelt's signing of Executive Order 9066 marked all Japanese residents and Japanese Americans as targets of hatred. While growing up not having to think explicitly about how race shaped their lives, Nisei were suddenly thrust into a situation where their racial identity became a major determining factor for exclusion. Within a few months' time, their schools, homes, and all their belongings had to be abandoned for a tenuous life behind barbed wire. This disjunction in their home and school life created a dissonance with which these students were forced to grapple. The internalized grief Nisei students had to bear was slightly relieved by the opportunity for some to express their thoughts in writing. Their pithy phrases, transcribed in exact form to the original, allude to their unswerving loyalty to the government and to their rights as citizens in a democracy. On a deeper level are the concerns raised by Nisei at the thought of having to leave their home—the place of their birth and the place where they made friends in their neighborhood schools.

Mar. 25, 42
Dear Miss Evanson,
    I am sorry we are leaving because I have first became acquainted with this school. I will always remember this school and teachers as one of the best.
Sincerely,
Mary

March 29, 1942
Dear Miss Evanson,

We are leaving our city, to where I am going I am wholly ignorant. However I am not unhappy, nor do I have objections for as long as this evacuation is for the benefit of the United State. But I do am regreting about leaving this school and the thought that I shall not see for a long while pains me extremely. Your pleasant ways of teaching had made my heart yearn for the days when I was in your classroom. Your kind smile and your wonderful work you did for me shall be one of my pleasant memories.

Tooru (8B4)

Mar. 25, 1942
Dear Miss Evanson,

Because of this war, we are asked to leave this city of Seattle. I am sure I will miss my teachers and Mr. Sears. There was never a school like Washington, and I will sure miss it. I will miss you very much. You have been very kind and patient throughout my years.

Sincerely Yours,
Masaharu (7A1)

Mar. 20, 1942
Dear Miss Evanson,

I well start out my letter by writing about the worst thing. I do not want to go away but the goverment says we all have to go so we have to mind him. It said in the Japanese paper that we have to go east of the cascade mt. but we were planning to go to Idaho or Montana.

Now that the war is going on many Japanese men, women, and girls are out of jobs. And a lot of my friends fater are in consentration camp. If I go there I hope I well have a teacher just like you. And rather more I hope the war well be strighten out very soon so that I would be able to attend Washington school.

Sincerely Yours
Sadako (7B1)

March 31, 1942
Dear Miss Evanson,

I am sorry we have to leave. Just when I was going to graduate Washington School. I'm glad that I had you in the 7B & A & 8B. I hope we do not have to go. Where ever I am going I wish I have a teacher like you. I enjoyed being in your room very much. When I go away I will always think about the wonderful time I had in Washington School. In so many month I wish the war will be over. I will always remember you.

Your pupil,
Martha (8A1)

4/2/41
Dear Miss Evanson,

I'm very sorry to leave Seattle. I shall miss all my friends. I enjoyed being in your room in the 7B4. I shall miss you and all the rest.

With Love,
Kazuko (8B5)

Mar. 25, 1942
Dear Miss Evanson,

I feel very said beacuse I have to leave such a nice school and all the helpful teachers especially you. I have been interested in history about Gods and Goddesses. When I first started to learn and read about them it seemed interesting and began to like it.

When I first started school I was about 5 (five) years of age. I haven't stayed once, took a double in fourth grade, and haven't took me since. I am eleven now and am going to be twelve this year on May ? (so and so). I hope to come back to Seattle after this awful war.

A pupil,
Reiko (7B3)

4/3/42
Dear Miss Evanson,

I am very lonely without your face smiling before us. I miss you very much but I hope to come back soon.

Your former pupil,
Katsuko

March 25, 194[2]
Dear Miss Evanson,

I am sorry that we will all be leaving the Washington School, but even though we are I will think about the ways we have been taught. I appreciated the way you and the teachers have been working with us.
Sincerely,
Yeoko (7B3)

Mar. 25 1942
Dear Miss Evanson,

I am very sorry I will have to leave Washington School so soon. As long as I am here I will try in some way to appreciate what you've taught me.

We all hope we will win this war (not the Japs) and come back to Seattle for more education.
Sincerely Yours,
James
7B3 Washington School

Dear Miss Evanson

My heart is so sad to have to leave this school and all the helpful teachers I had, one of whom I liked the best, Miss Evanson. I hope I may come sometime soon to visit the "Dear Old Washington School."
Sincerely,
Aido
7B4-8A6

Mar. 19, 1942
Dear Miss Evanson,

I am writing to you today because I am expecting to move away with in very short time. As you always know the japanese people has been asked by our goverment to evacuate. I do not know yet where we will go. I hope there will be some good school in which I can continual, my school work. I am very sorry to leave Seattle and Washington School. And most especially to lose you for my teacher. I am hoping the war trouble will be soon over and I could come back to Seattle and be in your school and have you for my teacher again.
Sincerely yours,
Chiyoko (7B1)

March 25, 1942
Dear Miss Evanson,

I am awfully sorry I am leaving, just when I was getting aquinted with the children and work. I would like all of you to write to me. This has been and will be always my favorite school.

For Get Me Not.

Sincerely,

Mary (7B1)

March 20, 1942
Dear Miss Evanson,

I am very sorry that I will soon be leaving Washington School and the teachers I have. As you know we have been asked to evacuate. My parents still haven't decided where to go. Where I am going I hope there will be a school like Washington School. I also hope to have a good teacher like you. I don't want to leave Seattle because I have been in Seattle from the time I was a little baby. I hate to lose you for my teacher and Mr. Sears as my principal. I know I am going to miss everybody. I am hoping the trouble will be over soon so we will not have to evacuate.

Sincerely,

Yurido (7B1)

Dear Miss Evanson:

Since we must leave Seattle and move to the east[1] I won't forget Washington School and its patient teachers and principal. I was born in Seattle and I wish it not to perish with bombs and bullets. And if Freedom and Liberty should fall it should grow again.

Don't forget, Buy United States Saving Stamps and bonds!

Sincerely Yours,

Tokunari

Dear Miss Evanson,

I have missed seeing your smiling face and I will miss you more, after all of us are gone. I enjoyed being in your class a year ago.

With love,

Hisako

April 3, 1942
Dear Miss Evanson,

I cannot express the way I enjoyed being one of your formal pupils. I am sorry because I have to leave Washington School and miss you and Mr. Sears and all the teachers. I like to write to my favorite teacher but the time is getting short and I must close this letter.

Respectfully yours,
Kazuo

March 24, 42
Dear Miss Evanson,

Because of this situation, we are asked to leave this dear city of Seattle and its surroundings. I am sure I will miss my teachers and Mr. Sears. There was never a school like Washington School and I sure will miss it. As for me, the one I will miss most will be you. You have been very patient and kind throughout my work. If the school I will attend next would have a teacher like you I will be only too glad. When I am on my way my memories will flow back to the time I was attending this school and the assemblies which were held in the hall.

Wherever I go I will be a loyal American
Love,
Emiko (7B1)

April 17, 1942
Dear Miss Evanson,

It makes me sad to write in this book for it will mean departure.

I hate to be leaving Seattle, for I'll not see my friends, nor my school but there is nothing I (we) or anyone can do about it.

I have enjoyed being a pupil of yours very much.

Sincerely,
Ai (8A5)

Mar. 25, 1942
Dear Miss Evanson,

When the time come for the Japanses people to move out of Seattle it will be hard to go because I was born here. But I will not forget the teacher of my old school and Washington School because they are so kind and I learn many things from them. I wish I can find some teacher that was as nice as you teachers was.

I am a American.

Sincerely Yours,

Haruo (7B1)

Mar. 24, 1942

Dear Miss Evanson,

I am very said we are leaving Washington School with all it's helpful teachers. I will always think of the happy times we had. I hope we have a good school and a teacher like you wherever we go. Whenever I think of Seattle I will think of you and all the teachers.

Sincerely yours,

Kazuko (7B3)

Mar. 23, 1942

Dear Miss Evanson

I am sorry we have to evacuate because I will miss my studies, teacher's, friend's and our principal, Mr. Sears.

Maybe it is better for us to go and do what the government says. I hope there is a school where I can continuie with my studies.

As you know Seattle is my home town so I am sorry to leave here. I hope this war will soon be over because then I could come back and to attend the Dear Old Washington School.

Yours truly,

Kazuko (7B1)

While the depth and complexity of what is written in the Nisei students' farewell messages are not immediately apparent, these passages provide critical insights into how they viewed citizenship, democracy, and America. At the same time, however, the students' American identity is overlapped and layered with their specific cultural experiences as Japanese Americans. The salient themes in these letters reflect the complex nature of their multiple and sedimented identities.[2]

One of the themes emerging from these letters is a collective sense of "we-ness" in the writings. The typical farewell begins with "I am sorry we are leaving." The "we" may be referring to the students' families, the Japanese American students, and/or the Japanese American community. "We" is not specified. An immediate analysis of the "we" issue might indicate some aspects of the cultural values of the Japanese American community in stressing a collective and cohesive group identity over individual identity. Whereas the students are individually "sorry" for leaving, they realize it is a particular "we" group that is leaving—a group that has become the focus of governmental exclusionary policies.

Many students phrased their departure in terms of "we are asked to leave Seattle." Using the word "ask" suggests that the evacuation was performed on a voluntary basis. Indeed, the government did "ask" for volunteer evacuation in the beginning but soon changed to a policy of forced removal. Nikkei, by and large, knew that they did not have a choice in the matter. Government newsreels of the time reflected the image of a "benevolent" bureaucracy helping to find a "safe" place for Japanese residents and citizens, and perhaps that ideal was accepted to varying degrees by Japanese and non-Japanese alike. This acceptance may explain some of the students' writings in that particular tone.

Although loyalty is not often explicitly stated by the students, evidence of loyalty on the part of Japanese Americans is apparent. For example, a student wrote, "However I am not unhappy nor do I have objections for as long as this evacuation is for the benefit of the United State [sic]." Likewise, another expressed similar sentiments: "I do not want to go away but the goverment [sic] says we all have to go so we have to mind him." Additional excerpts also contain important clues. A student wrote, "It makes me sad to write in this book for it will mean departure. I hate to be leaving Seattle, for I'll not see my friends, nor my school but there is nothing I (we) or anyone can do about it." Perhaps because of the hopelessness of the situation, the students felt they had no other choice but to do what the government said. Loyalty, in this manner, was more like obeisance. They were maintaining loyalty to a government that held them suspect. So in an effort to be loyal, they had to do what the government ordered. Another student remarked, "I am sorry we have to evacuate because I will miss my studies, teachers, friends, and our principal, Mr. Sears. Maybe it's better for us to go and do what the government says. I hope there is a school where I can continuie [*sic*] my studies." To perceive a "general acceptance" on the part of Seattle's Nikkei may be to misunderstand the cultural sentiment of *shikata ga-nai*, "it cannot be helped."

Loyalty had been a component of Americanization and citizenship education in the Seattle schools since 1916. While the thrust of the 1930s and 1940s lay more with tolerance and interculturalism, loyalty and patriotism were an aspect of the students' civic education. At the community level, older Nisei who were involved with the Japanese American Citizens' League (JACL) stressed the importance of loyalty and patriotism to the U.S. government, especially during this time of forced evacuation. While dissident voices in the Nikkei community questioned the extent to which their loyalty was taken seriously, the public image to project was one of trust toward the government. After all, they were American citizens—or were they?

The "we-ness" and loyalty, alongside the evacuation's throwing into question their sense of identity, created a dissonance. One student mentioned instances where many Japanese men, women, and girls lost jobs. Indeed, in the Seattle schools, Japanese American school clerks were terminated from employment as prejudice against Nikkei grew. While the college students at the University of Washington condemned the effort of a small, elite group of white mothers to oust Nisei school employees, the damage had already been done. To show loyalty to the war effort, a number of Japanese American workers resigned, upon which one of the "Westgate mothers" quipped, "I think that's very white of those girls."[3]

As a further sign of loyalty, in addition to acting "white," students began to distinguish themselves from the Japanese in Japan. The emphatic tone in James's letter is clear: "We all hope we will win this war (not the Japs) and come back to Seattle for more education." There was no reason to doubt

James, as he was born in Seattle and the United States was his home. But his parenthetical "not the Japs" remark reveals his need to make that distinction known to the reader, by using the mainstream, pejorative term for the Japanese at the time. His assertion of his American identity is also poignantly expressed by other students' phrases: "Wherever I go I will be a loyal American" and "I am a[n] American." For many generations, Japanese Americans had fought for recognition and viable rights as American citizens. Their continuous efforts, despite racist governmental policies of the past, to voice their loyalty to the United States had gone unheard.

Moreover, the students were making the point that they were all American citizens despite that fact that they had to leave. The Nisei's assertion of their American identities was made more explicit at a time when their status as American citizens was called into question. The students' need to reinforce their identities meant that their identities were held suspect. Several students remarked that they did not wish to leave because they had been born in Seattle and leaving their homes would sadden them deeply ("I don't want to leave Seattle because I have been in Seattle from the time I was a little baby"). Another student wrote, "I was born in Seattle and I wish it not to perish with bombs and bullets." The beginning of one message, "When the time comes for the Japanses [*sic*] people to move out of Seattle, it will be hard to go because I was born here," typifies the general feeling of having to leave a place of one's birth. Reiterating the fact that people born in the United States have automatic citizenship, based upon the principle of jus soli, was possibly one of the lessons learned in Ella Evanson's social studies class as well as in the assemblies conducted by the principal, Arthur Sears. To be sure, the trauma of having to move from one's home as an adolescent heightened anxieties even more.

In spite of feeling uncertain about their futures, the students revealed their appreciation for their school and their teachers, especially Ella Evanson. Even with the interruption caused by an extreme circumstance in their lives, schooling remained vital to them. To conceive of a future without schools was unimaginable. The message of wanting to be in school and with former classmates occurred time and time again in the students' letters to Evanson from Camp Harmony in Puyallup, Washington.[4]

NON-NISEI REFLECTIONS ON THE EVE
OF THEIR CLASSMATES' INCARCERATION

How much did the news of the incarceration affect the lives of non-Nisei students? Were they at all attempting to reconcile the conflicts between the ideals of democracy and the reality of racism? While these questions might tempt one to conduct a psychosocial analysis, they are nevertheless important to consider in grasping what the "Japanese evacuation" meant for non-Nisei students.

The writings by non-Nisei students on the impending incarceration show a range of emotions, from sadness to indifference and from citizenship to racial identification. The forced removal is couched in terms of "safety for their own good" and assurance that the government would "take care of them." Perhaps influenced by popular media, such as the newspapers, radio, or newsreels, or by national, local, or parental attitudes, some of the students rationalized the "evacuation." While it is impossible to gather the totality and depth of what the students felt, the following writings provide powerful clues.

JUNE—ENGLISH 7B3—APRIL 24, 1942
THE JAPANESE EVACUATION

We are all sorry to see the Japanese leave for we know if they do not have that the white people who don't like the behavor of Japan will start beating up on the American Japanese so that is why they are leaving.

I hope some day after the war is all over the Japanese that were evacuated can come back.

One of my best girl friends is leaving today to a more safer place.

At Washington the 8A girls and one class from the 7B-7A, 8B put on a dance this was a farewell party for the Japanese who were leaving.

I think that it is best for them to leave and go to a much safer place in land.

LAMAR—ENGLISH 7B3—APRIL 24, 1942
JAPANESE EVACUATION

The japanese have to all be out of Seattle by May 1. I do not feel very said about it, although there are some good japanese in the city. The children in my room that are japanese are leaving. We have one Chinese girl called Helen[5] in our room. I just recently found out she was Chinese, I always thought she was Japanese.

JACK

Today Washington school boys and girls gave a farwell to the Japanese boy and girl. We are very sory thay have to leave and we all are very sory and sad. Thay have shown the best of sitizzonship in every way and everything thay have done.

LOUISE—ENGLISH 7B3—APRIL 24, 1942
THE JAPANESE EVACUATION

This week the Japanese are going and I will miss them very much. Mary and Dorothy were my best friends and they are going. It is very unhappy for they are going and we wish they could stay.

MR. DON—ENGLISH 7B3—APRIL 24, 1942
JAPANESE EVACUATION

I dont think I like the Evacuation becaus the Japanese when they get where they are going they won't have no friends or anything to do. They won't get any privlages of the Americans. They won't be able to see a movie or nothing else like that. I think they should have the privileges of the Americans because there just as good citizens as we are.

DORIS
THE DEPARTURE[6]

I am very sorry that the japanese children are leaving Washington school. They were really good friends to all of us American children even though there American citizens, too.

I am very sorry to see some of my best friends go which I have first got aqquainted with this semester. It was really a pleasure.

I am going to try if I can to get their autugraphs or picture of them so I can remember them always.

JAPANESE EVACUATION[7]

For some I am glad, some sorry. I know some J. boys that would punch holes in tires and break windows if you ask them to. Other are real nice people. They have manners and sometimes are considered better Am. cit. than most white people. Ernest

MARSHA—ENGLISH 7B3—APRIL 24, 1942
JAPANESE EVACUATION

The Japanese people are going to leave us soon. We are all wishing that they could stay. Some are going today and others after ward. In Washington School all the Japanese are very nic. The Chinese and japanese never qurral or fight and they are good sports. In our room all of us like all of the Japanese pupils. Some are going to Idaho Falls, Montana, and other places.

GRACE
JAPANESE EVACUATION

After all we're all Americans but the children with Japanese ancestors will have to be evacuated.

Washington school will not be the same soon because it will be much smaller. Many faces will be missing, to our dispare.

We are sorry to see the Japanese go.

MARJORIE
JAPANESE EVACUATION

I feal very sorry for the Japanese that have to go away. Some of my best friends are Japanese, but I'm sure that Our *Goverment* will take care of them, as they were here and we'll have a small school when the Japanese go away. We are sure that they're like it over there. It's very bueatiful there. My brothers has a farm over east of the mountain. And every summer I go there and may be I may see a few of my friend.

LEE ROY
THE JAPANESE EVACUATION

Some of the Japanese boys, and girls, of Washington, Jounior High School, are leaving us today. Some of them are leaving today, some monday, and the rest Tuesday. About 25 or 30 children are leaving today. They are going to go to a camp at Puyallup, which use to be a fair.

Today in our Assembly we had a fairwell party for the Japanese boy, and girls. The girls, and boys danced there. They danced to many songs.

I had a friend that is leaving today.

We were all very sad to see the Japanese children go today and the other days.

APRIL 24, 1942

Dear Mary,

I am sorry you have to leave us soon. I wish when you get to your new home that you will send me your address and write to me. I posted your picture in my book. When you get there send me some more.

Will you say hello to Ryko, Kazodo and Mary H. *Please.* Well I'll close.

Love Betty.

BOB
FAREWELL PARTY

Today we had a farewell party in honor of all the Japanese that will be leaving in the next few days. The different rooms did dances. The one I and almost everybody else thought was best were the dances put on by the 8-A dancing club.

    We are all sorry to see the Japanese go. I hope the war will soon end in our favor so that the Japanese will be able to come back to Seattle.

Many non-Nisei students, especially the female students, expressed concern and sadness at the thought of being forced to sever their friendships at school. Other students remarked how much the student body would change once their Nisei peers were gone. More than one-third of Washington school's population would disappear after May of 1942. At nearby Bailey Gatzert Elementary (from which a majority of Washington School Nisei came), the Asian student population constituted an overwhelming majority. The sea of empty desks after May 4 would be a constant reminder of missing classmates. Schooling would be disrupted on all fronts.

One can only surmise how the boys and girls interacted at the farewell party.[8] It was there perhaps that Ella Evanson, with her farewell book made for her by a student, had the idea to have all the Japanese American students write their farewell reflections. The songs and dances that filled the classroom perhaps hid the feelings of sorrow and uncertainty soon to follow. For one last moment, all the students of Washington were able to experience time together. Many non-Nisei students might have felt a little more at ease in the thought that the government would "take care" of Japanese Americans in providing "saftey for their own good." They believed in the benevolence of the government to act on behalf of all citizens. Regardless of their naive understandings, the next day and those to follow would affect everyone's life.[9]

While many students were sad, not all students felt that way. As one student wrote, "For some I am glad, for some I am sorry...." The probity of their remarks reveals, at least, that some students did hold negative feelings toward their Nisei classmates. On an essay written by Gerald, Ella Evanson's handwritten note claimed that he had been in a "knife incident" with

Hideo and friend. To be sure, conflicts between students and some occasional fights between boys, in particular, are to be expected and did in fact occur. However, even the ones not very sad to see their Japanese classmates leave did call them even "better citizens than the whites."

Lamar's letter raises a curiosity regarding the acknowledgment (or lack thereof) of different nationalities within Asian cultures. He realized for the first time that Helen was Chinese and not Japanese. Playing on the stereotype that all Asians look the same, the popular press began to provide derogatory caricatures for the mainstream public to distinguish between Chinese and Japanese individuals. But given the student's recent discovery of Helen's nationality, what was the practice at Washington School, in particular, and the Seattle Public Schools, in general, with regard to recognizing differences within racial groups? How progressive were their seemingly progressive pedagogies?

Some students affirmed the citizenship of their classmates with statements such as "Thay [sic] have shown the best of sitizzonship [sic] in every way and everything thay [sic] have done" and "They have manners and sometimes are considered better Am. cit. than most white people." Citizenship and citizenship education, in keeping with the tradition in the Seattle Public Schools' Americanization program, included an emphasis on loyalty.[10]

Another student's concern rested with his Nisei classmates' no longer being able to enjoy the everyday "rights" of "Americans" such as watching movies. Don's consideration for the daily activities his Nisei classmates would miss indicates that he was attempting to grasp what lay ahead for his school friends. He realized that the "privileges" of Americans should be open to all. He concluded his essay, however, with "because there [sic] just as good citizens as we are." Here an "us-them" distinction in citizenship indicates that an "American" is someone who is white. To be sure, the normative view of an America that is defined by whites was not new. Neither the school nor the friendships between white and Nisei schoolmates structurally changed that perspective. Grace's sentiment captures the contradiction and dissonance felt by many Nisei: "After all we're all Americans but the children with Japanese ancestors will have to be evacuated." Being a Japanese American held provisional citizenship status.

Specifically, the tenuous citizenship status meant being a "non-alien." With such play on words, Nisei were categorized as such and deemed unequal to (white) citizens—even though "non-alien" really meant citizen. Yoshiko Uchida's autobiography, *The Invisible Thread*, explains the situation quite dramatically:

> It was a sad day for all Americans of Japanese ancestry. Our government no longer considered us its citizens, simply referring to us as "non-aliens." It also chose to ignore the Fifth and Fourteenth Amendments to the Constitution that guaranteed "due process of law" and "equal protection under the law for all citizens." We were to be imprisoned in concentration camps without a trial or hearing of any kind.
>
> "But we're at war with Germany and Italy, too," I objected. "Why are only the Japanese Americans being imprisoned?"
>
> No one, including our government, had an answer for that.[11]

Indeed, language became a powerful tool for devising race-based policies of exclusion. For the Japanese, to be an American required that they be incarcerated behind barbed wire fences and salute the flag, expressing loyalty to a government that betrayed more than 120,000 of its residents. The oral history narrators' own analyses and responses to the students' writings later in chapter 6 indicate, too, that feelings of betrayal, confusion, and sorrow surrounded their everyday lives for the next three years.

In the following chapter I highlight the major historical events in Seattle that shaped the lives of Japanese immigrant Americans and how their permanent settlement in the premier city of the Pacific Northwest became dictated by policies beyond their control.

Chapter 2

SETTING THE STAGE:

SEATTLE'S JAPANESE AMERICA

BEFORE WORLD WAR II

★   ★   ★   ★   ★

Seattle, named after the chief of the Duwamish and Suquamish tribes, already existed in a complex cultural system established by American Indians—primarily the Nisqually, Snoqualmie, and Muckleshoot, in addition to the Duwamish and Suquamish—centuries before the arrival of its permanent white settlers from the Midwest in 1851. The pristine wilderness, the Puget Sound, the abundance of natural resources, and the consequent potential for the building of labor and industry lured prospectors to establish an economic base, and a new home, in the second-largest town (to Walla Walla) in the Washington Territory. As evidence of the sustained economic development, Seattle's population swelled past 230,000 from 1880 to 1910,[1] even after a devastating fire leveled much of downtown's Pioneer Square area in 1889. Such growth attracted transient workers along "Skid Row" and the more permanent settlers who established themselves as the new bourgeoisie in the affluent neighborhoods of West Seattle, Queen Anne, and Capital Hill.[2]

Pivotal to Seattle's boon were the contributions by the early Asian immigrants to the area. By 1880 Chinese immigrants numbered 3,176 in the Washington Territory, about 4 percent of the population. The majority of these early Asian settlers came in the late 1850s from the famine-stricken area of Guangdong (Kwantung) Province in southeast China near the port city of Guangzhou. They helped to build the western railroads and provided labor for many of the region's major industries as well as working as cooks, domestic servants, and laundrymen. Tales of gold and subsequent riches in Alaska and in the rivers of Oregon, Washington, and British Columbia initially drew a number of Chinese from California to the Pacific Northwest. Over time the Seattle Chinese established commercial and community ties in the southern end of downtown Seattle, currently known as the International District. However, the violent expulsion of Chinese in Seattle and Tacoma in the 1880s, following the 1882 Chinese Exclusion Act restricting immigration from China, curtailed the further development of a Chinese enclave in those areas. The labor shortage resulting from the expulsion of the Chinese led to growing opportunities for the newly arrived Japanese—Issei immigrants—and for a number of African Americans who moved to Seattle in large numbers after 1900.

The first Japanese immigration occurred in 1868 in Hawaii, due in large part to the Westernization of Japan under the Meiji Restoration in that same year. The sweeping social and economic changes—which included universal public education, national taxes, and a push for industrialization—took a toll on the large, rural peasant class. For some, the idea of leaving their homeland to embark on a new opportunity abroad and return with newly acquired wealth seemed attractive. As a result the large-scale immigration of Japanese to the U.S. mainland began in the 1890s and continued until 1907–1908, and to a very limited degree until 1924, when the Immigration Act was enacted. These new Asian immigrants found work on the railroads and in sawmills, logging camps, shipbuilding, and canneries throughout the Pacific Northwest.

A number of other Issei began cultivating land for agricultural production in the greater Seattle area. First working as seasonal laborers for paltry wages as in other industries, the Japanese farmers' ability to convert formerly unusable land for crops impressed their landowners. As a result landowners provided Japanese workers with reduced rent, enabling them to start farms. Soon afterward Issei farmers began to establish a co-op system through *tanomoshi* clubs—lending money to members on a rotating basis—to aid one another's farming ventures. The Pike Place Market, now a popular tourist destination, became the site where, by World War I, Japanese farmers occupied an overwhelming 70 percent of the market stalls selling their produce. Some estimate that in the 1920s Japanese supplied 75 percent of the region's vegetables and half the milk. In spite of their gains in crop development and production, many faced anti-Asian attitudes and structural racial discrimination. The passage of the 1921 Alien Land Law by the Washington State Legislature, following California's lead, not only forbade the sale of land to "aliens ineligible to citizenship" but also restricted leasing or renting land and renewing of old leases. This was one of many restrictions placed on Asians in general and Japanese in particular in their attempts to eke out a living. Japanese all along the West Coast of the United States suffered a similar fate.

IMMIGRATION RESTRICTIONS AND ANTI-JAPANESE ACTIVITIES

Discriminatory policies in immigration and citizenship can be traced back to the Naturalization Act of 1790, providing for naturalization of "any alien, being a free white person."[3] After a revision of the statute post–Civil War, it prohibited any Chinese immigrant from becoming an American citizen, and in 1922 the Supreme Court interpreted the statute to prohibit the naturalization of any "Oriental."[4] A majority of the Japanese immigrants landed in California, and that was where the spectacle of anti-Japanese efforts took place.

In May 1905, delegates from sixty-seven organizations met in San Francisco to form the Asiatic Exclusion League, later to become the Japanese Exclusion League.[5] Their racial and economic motivations to exclude Japanese took the form of legislation, boycott, school segregation, and propaganda. By 1908 the league had more than 100,000 members and 238 affiliated groups, mostly labor unions. Clearly, the presence of Japanese immigrants posed an economic threat to the group members, primarily

European immigrants. Even nonmembers expressed support for the league's actions.

An important and pivotal move in the anti-Japanese campaign came in the proposal to segregate Japanese schoolchildren in the San Francisco schools. On December 11, 1906 the school board issued an order barring Asian children from white primary schools, even though they had been legally excluded since the 1850s. This move, backed by a coalition of labor unions and politicians, affected only ninety-three Japanese students, twenty-five of them born in the United States, who were then in the San Francisco Public Schools.

The news reached Japan of the San Francisco School Board decision, and President Theodore Roosevelt, in an attempt to avoid conflicts with Japan, struck a deal: in return for the board's rescission of its order, he would negotiate with Japan to restrict immigration. Thus was born the Gentlemen's Agreement of 1907 whereby Japan agreed not to issue more workers' passports valid for the continental United States, and to restrict issuance to "laborers who have already been in America and to the parents, wives and children of laborers already resident there."[6] This limited the entry of Japanese immigrants between 1908 and 1924. Between 1900 and 1920 many men summoned wives from Japan who entered immigrant society in one of three ways: (1) as wives who were left behind in Japan by immigrant males; (2) as women who married single men after they returned to Japan to seek brides; and (3) through the "picture bride" practice.[7]

In conjunction with immigration restrictions came serious economic sanctions. The 1913 California Alien Land Law barred future land purchases by aliens ineligible for citizenship and forbade such aliens to acquire leases for periods longer than three years. As a response to the racist policy, some resident Japanese purchased land under their children's names, with the parents serving as guardians over the land. But that was soon overturned in a 1920 amendment prohibiting any further transfer of land to Japanese nationals, forbidding them to lease land, barring any corporation in which Japanese held a majority of stock from lease or purchase of land, and pro-

TABLE 2.1:
SEATTLE'S ETHNIC MINORITY POPULATION, 1900-1940

	1900	1910	1920	1930	1940
Black	406	2,296	2,894	3,303	3,789
Japanese	2,900	6,127	7,874	8,448	6,975
Chinese	438	924	1,351	1,347	1,781
Filipino	—	—	458	1,614	1,392
Native American	22	24	106	172	222
White	76,815	227,753	302,580	350,639	354,101
Other	—	70	49	60	42
Total	80,671	237,194	315,312	365,583	368,302

Source: Quintard Taylor, *The Forging of a Black Community: Seattle's Central District from 1870 through the Civil Rights Era* (Seattle: University of Washington Press, 1994), 108.

hibiting immigrant parents from serving as guardians for their minor children. In Washington State, the Alien Land Law enacted in March 1921 also aimed squarely at aliens who were ineligible for citizenship.[8] By 1924 the anti-Japanese attack, not only in California but in various West Coast areas, had achieved the complete exclusion of immigration from Japan.

It is through these various immigration restrictions that the distinctive generations in the Japanese American community developed. The limited influx of Japanese women's immigration, during the time of the Gentlemen's Agreement up to 1924, marked the period in which the Nisei generation burgeoned. To be sure, California's nativist measures directly influenced the everyday realities for Seattle's Nikkei, the city's largest ethnic minority group from 1900 to before the Second World War.

Amid racial hostilities, however, Issei were able to find ways to work within the racist system and transmit cultural values to Nisei, syncretizing the moral aspects of their Japanese and newly adopted "American" cultures.

SEATTLE'S JAPANESE AMERICA

An area of approximately four blocks southeast of downtown Seattle made up *Nihonmachi*, or Japantown. As with the early Chinese residents and African Americans, Issei were restricted by racial covenants to create their own business and community centers only from South King Street to north of Yesler Way. The heart of Nihonmachi was situated on Sixth Avenue and Main Street. Hotels, Japanese restaurants, barbershops, labor contractor offices, Japanese dancing schools, and the Buddhist temple lined the streets providing livelihood and a sense of community to its local residents. The second-generation Japanese, Nisei, grew up combining the cultural influences of their parents with their "American" culture of bobby socks and baseball caps, and their segregated boys' and girls' clubs. Many of their cultural events, both Japanese and American, took place in the Nippon Kan Theater, the primary community center. The "typical average" Nisei was born between 1918 and 1922 to a thirty-five-year-old father and a twenty-five-year-old mother, reaching legal age between 1939 and 1943.[9] By the 1930s the Nisei generation, an overwhelming majority being children, predominated. By the decade's end, the children outnumbered their Issei parents.[10]

In characterizing the cultural traits of Seattle's Nikkei, the sociologist S. Frank Miyamoto contends that two major values aided in the Issei's instillation of ethnic pride in their children:

> First, the Japanese immigrants brought from Japan and transmitted to their children cultural values, consistent with and complementary to the middle-class values emphasized in American society, which emphasized status achievement.
>
> Second, the Japanese minority maintained a high degree of family and community organization in America, and these organizations enforced value conformity and created conditions and means for status achievement.[11]

In addition, the cohesiveness of family, extended family groups, quasi-familial relations (between neighbors and prefectural organizations), various community organizations, and the disposition to work together as a group all played a part.[12] The Issei brought the values with which they were familiar from living in Japan during the Meiji Era—one of them calling for a universal education system whereby the moral script of loyalty played a major role. These all contributed to the Japanese American community's high degree of the persistence before and after World War II.

Despite the existence of the language barrier between the first and second generation many Issei transmitted cultural values and concepts through what Miyamoto calls the "paratactic mode,"[13] which stressed learning through observation and experience. The paratactic mode worked to transmit many parental attitudes, sentiments, and values. Among the major cultural values were respect for etiquette, regard for status and authority, and attentiveness to principles of social obligation. This brief examination into the major cultural values is not intended to essentialize the experiences of all Japanese Americans. Rather, I wish to highlight the ways in which their lives were fashioned by some of the overarching cultural constructs in which they were embedded.

The ethical system of norms, *On*, *Giri*, *Ninjo*, and *Enryo*,[14] influenced by the long religious and cultural tradition—syncretizing Shinto, Buddhist, and Neo-Confucianist thought—during Japan's Tokugawa period figured significantly in modes of cultural transmission by Issei to Nisei.[15] *On*, which is ascribed obligation, comes from Confucianism and marks an individual's duties to parents, family, country, and teachers, for example. It is a value to which one is born and cannot ignore. *Giri*, contractual obligation, is one that is incurred and achieved and built into every form of relationship. *Ninjo*, humane sensibility, seeks to achieve sensitivity with others to a high degree. It is a form of extreme empathy. Lastly, *Enryo* refers to modesty and requires an exercise of excessive restraint. One must initially hold back and hesitate. *Enryo* is regarded as explaining much of Japanese American behavior, particularly in reference to one's seeming indifferent and deferring opinions, when in fact these are signs of respect. Generally, these norms hold the orientation of the group over the needs of the individual. One is always in relation to an other.[16] The most persistent efforts at training were devoted to teaching Nisei the ancient principles of *ko* (duty to parent), *on* (filial obligation of reciprocity), and *giri* (duty and responsibility). The extent to which Nisei truly internalized these values is questionable, as the degree of parental influence also differed. But clearly the emphasis on these traits and their daily lives in Nihonmachi where they were often practiced, left an indelible mark on Nisei.

EDUCATION

The influence of education and its role in the formation of Japanese American cultural values cannot be overlooked. On the whole, education in the social and cultural uplift of ethnic minority and immigrant groups in the United States has been a means of establishing structural equality. Struggles against inferior and segregated education have been well documented. And to suggest that *only* Asian Americans value education undermines the long history of resistance fought by parents from *all* minority groups on behalf of their children, and only perpetuates the myth of Asians as "model minorities." Thus, it is important to remember that Issei parents' concern for their children's education reflected a larger pattern of minority parental advocacy, with their unique experience being framed within the cultural traditions emanating from Japan.

JAPANESE LANGUAGE SCHOOLS

Realizing the widening gulf between the generations, especially in maintaining traditional Japanese customs, Seattle's Issei parents established a Japanese Language School, Nihongo Gakko, in 1902, the first of its kind on the West Coast.[17] At its peak over two thousand students attended Nihongo Gakko every weekday for an hour and a half after their regular public school. Most Nisei attended Japanese Language Schools for eight years and did not learn past the rudiments of the Japanese alphabet system.[18]

The initial intent in establishing Japanese Language Schools throughout the West Coast lay in preparing Nisei to attend public schools in Japan, based on a traditional custom of *dekasegi*.[19] Many parents felt that the possession of dual citizenship by Nisei afforded them the right and privilege to an education in Japan. Having been born in the United States, Nisei were American citizens according to the principle of jus soli. In addition, Nisei with Japanese fathers had automatic Japanese citizenship, based on the principle of jus sanguinis. But after continued deliberation on the racial problems that might ensue for Nisei in the matter of their dual citizenship, as seen from the perspective of the white majority, members of the Japanese community elected to educate their children for permanent residence in the United States, thus eliminating in their view the whites' assertions that Nisei would hold divided loyalties. The petitioning and lobbying efforts of Issei and Nisei from Seattle and Los Angeles resulted in the Japanese Diet's amendment to the Japanese Nationality Act in 1916. This amendment allowed the parents or guardians of Nisei who were fourteen years old or younger to renounce their offsprings' Japanese citizenship on their behalf; it also allowed those Nisei who were fifteen to sixteen years old to renounce it themselves. Male Nisei seventeen years old or older could forswear their Japanese citizenship only if they had fulfilled their military obligation. This did not pose too big a challenge since the majority of Nisei males were relatively young.

This move to settle the duality question further emphasized the function of Japanese Language Schools to educate Nisei for a permanent life in the United States:

> The main objective will be to educate future permanent residents of the United States; and Recognizing the necessity of an American education, Japanese schools will provide supplementary instruction in Japanese and education about Japan.[20]

This resolution, adopted in 1912 at a conference of the Japanese Association of America, shows the long-standing concern of Japanese community members for the education of Nisei and their acculturation into the American public schools. Despite growing suspicion and opposition by whites, because the Japanese Language Schools promoted loyalty to Japan, educators and parents aimed to achieve the opposite.

SEATTLE PUBLIC SCHOOLS

Racial covenants in housing and the resulting de facto segregation in public schools delimited Nisei attendance to those schools bordering their neighborhoods. Prior to the Civil Rights Act of 1964, many ethnic minorities were not able to set up residence beyond the prescribed boundaries. Desegregation in the 1970s, with voluntary busing programs, allowed for more movement of minorities and whites into certain schools. So for many Seattle schoolchildren prior to the 1960s, their lives existed within the boundaries of their neighborhoods and did not extend much further.

The Seattle Public Schools, through Americanization and citizenship education,[21] were the primary force of acculturation for Nisei.[22] The Seattle school system, established in 1870, was based on the idea of a neighborhood community school where more emphasis was placed on transmitting academic content and developing intellectual skills, character, morality, and good citizenship than on job preparation.[23] The district's transformation into a major urban system began in 1901 when Frank B. Cooper became the school district's superintendent. Most of Seattle's Nisei went to school under the leadership of Cooper.

Between the 1910s and the 1920s the Main Street School (later moved and renamed Bailey Gatzert), Pacific School, Central School, and Washington School, located east of Nihonmachi, became sites where large numbers of Nisei first experienced their entrée into school culture. Main Street School was closest to the heart of where Nikkei lived. Washington School was closer to the Central District of Seattle where many southern European and Jewish immigrants presided.

Prior to the 1920s, the Main Street School with Ada Mahon as the principal was the local community school for Nisei. Bailey Gatzert, a new, larger structure, was built in 1921 where Mahon continued to serve as the principal. As described in the *Histories of Seattle Public Schools*: "So it was that on a rainy day in December, 1921, Ida [sic] Mahon led her students and teachers on a damp march up Jackson Street to a new building at Twelfth South and Weller Street."[24] By 1929 the school required an expansion of a new gymnasium, teachers' room, music room, science room, art room, library, and two new classrooms. According to the report, the children attending were of Chinese and Japanese ancestry before the Second World War and the development of a new housing project along Yesler Way resulted in the "world's three major races" being "represented in nearly equal portions" by 1960.[25]

Before 1942, Asian students indeed predominated at Bailey Gatzert. By 1920 the student body at Bailey Gatzert consisted primarily of Japanese and

Chinese students. Table 2.2 represents, in descending order, the number of Japanese and Nisei students in the Seattle Public Grade Schools for the 1920–1921 academic year, the only years between 1916 and 1941 in which full student data are available.

Main Street School contained the largest contingent of Japanese American students. The school was in the hub of Seattle's Japantown. Racial covenants and school segregation created the distinct ethnic neighborhoods in central and south Seattle. The student enrollment at Main Street School was 452 in 1921; 445, or 99 percent, of those students being of Chinese and Japanese descent (25 and 74 percent, Chinese and Japanese, respectively).[26] For Washington School, the percentage of Nikkei students was far less, 5 percent. The highest attendance at Washington School for the 1920–1921 academic year was 756.[27] Many of the Nisei students whose writings are represented in this book attended Bailey Gatzert for elementary schooling, prior to being transferred to Washington School for the seventh and eighth grades.

As Bailey Gatzert's most memorable principal, Mahon is often described as a "strict, no-nonsense kind of teacher who emphasized traditional values in school instruction, [and] was considered by the Japanese community a most admirable head."[28] The Issei certainly were most appreciative of Mahon's efforts to instill ethics of hard work in schooling and for building moral character.[29] To show the Japanese community's deep gratitude for Mahon's leadership role, a group of Issei raised funds to provide Mahon with a tour of Japan and a large reception in her honor prior to her departure.[30] Issei parents also provided and paid for a trip to Japan for Arthur Sears, principal of Washington School, and J. M. Widmer, principal of Central School.[31] Part of Mahon's success is attributed to the fact that her student body was overwhelmingly Japanese.[32] The homogenous population, in addition to the cultural values shared by the Japanese in Seattle, bolstered Mahon's ability to be a stern and authoritative leader, a quality seemingly admired by Issei parents.

TABLE 2.2:
SEATTLE GRADE SCHOOLS WITH THE HIGHEST NUMBERS OF JAPANESE,
1920–1921

Schools	"Colored"	Chinese	Japanese
Main Street	1	111	334
Pacific	24	34	164
Central	2	30	82
Washington	3	3	36
Hawthorne	5	2	22
South Park	0	0	17
Beacon Hill	0	1	12
Seward	0	1	11
Lowell	4	0	10
Rainier	24	6	10
Concord	0	0	8
Stevens, I. I.	0	4	8
Denny	1	1	7
Minor, T. T.	5	1	6
Summit	9	3	6
Cascade	0	0	5
Ravenna	1	0	5
University Heights	0	1	5
Walla Walla	10	0	5
Columbia	4	0	4
Madrona	0	0	4
West Queen Anne	0	0	4
Fairview	0	0	3
Gatewood	0	0	3
Hay, John	0	0	3
Muir, John	1	0	3
Total for Grades	252	208	803

Source: *Thirty-fourth Annual Report of the Public Schools, 1916–1921* (Seattle: Seattle Public Schools, 1921), 226–227. The information provided is not a complete listing of all Seattle grade schools for 1920–1921.

Even for older Nisei today the legend of Ada Mahon lives. A Bailey Gatzert graduate reflected on Mahon's philosophy of equality in the midst of war and how she worked at every level to provide an environment of intercultural appreciation:

Each spring, Bailey Gatzert Elementary School's departing sixth-grade class was called to the auditorium stage for traditional "moving up" ceremonies. As the rest of the students loudly kept count, each class member stepped off the stage to receive a firm, farewell handshake from Principal Ada J. Mahon.

Although Miss Mahon never had children of her own, thousands of Seattle-area youngsters growing up in pre-World War II Chinatown and the "Nihon-machi" (Japan Town) areas were her legacy. She was "Irish tough" and proud, teaching her "children" to have the same tenacity and pride about being Asian, Native American or black.

Her influence extended well beyond her school property at 12th and Weller streets. Miss Mahon was social worker, counselor, cop, judge and jury—and was loved and respected.

The Asian parents held her in awe. With their strong cultural belief in education as the path to success, the parents entrusted Miss Mahon to build the bridge for their children. Among the Issei (first-generation Japanese immigrants) parents, who hold teachers in high esteem, she was "Mahon Sensei."

Miss Mahon served as the cultural and generational intermediary as we struggled with our "Americanization" process, which sometimes clashed with our parents' cultural traditions. She prepared us to succeed in an adult world where we would be considered minorities.

The world turned topsy-turvey on Dec. 7, 1941. The next morning, after the Japanese attack on Pearl Harbor, we were immediately directed to the school auditorium. Miss Mahon, looking out to her sea of colored faces, began the assembly, leading us in the Pledge of Allegiance.

The usually composed Miss Mahon shook with emotion. "You are all my children. Although we come from different places and may look different, we are the same," Miss Mahon said, her voice breaking at times. She warned that friendships would be tested and that difficult times loomed ahead.

In early spring, school enrollment began dropping as the students of Japanese ancestry left in compliance with the wartime evacuation orders. Miss Mahon held special assemblies, timed with their departures, calling them to the stage, so everyone could say goodbye. The ceremony, usually reserved for sixth-graders moving on to Washington junior high school, was modified to include all students who were leaving with their parents to the internment camps.

On a bright spring day in May, I passed through Bailey Gatzert's large double doors for the last time. My last glimpse of Miss Mahon was her standing ramrod straight and resolute on the front steps. One hand—always extended to help and sometimes holding a wooden ruler to discipline—was waving goodbye, and the other clutched a white tear-soaked handkerchief.[33]

Mahon was revered and cherished by the Nikkei community. Her authoritative leadership style, balanced by a sensitivity toward those in the Nikkei community, earned the respect of her students and their parents. Pride in one's ethnicity and heritage, while holding steadfast to the ideals of Americanism through the melting pot ideal, was the foundation of her democratic beliefs. Within her sphere of influence, Mahon managed to control the level of external pressures brought on by the war.

Yet the intrusion of everyday politics in the daily activities of school forced Mahon to confront the issue of how the war would affect more than half of her student body. The majority Nisei student body at Bailey Gatzert needed a school leader to set a moral tone above the clangor of hatred. She, as well as Arthur Sears, principal of Washington School, stressed the ideals of an equal, "American" identity against the backdrop of a society that began to question Nikkei's loyalty to the United States.[34]

How and in what ways did the Seattle Public Schools begin to lay the foundation for such a view of democracy and citizenship? The following two chapters illuminate the Seattle schools' approach to democratic citizenship education and how its principals and teachers worked to impart such ideals to their students from 1916 to 1942. As the years progressed and as the war drew on, such lessons on the value of equality and democracy became even more pronounced for Seattle's Nisei students.

Chapter 3

LOOKING BACKWARD:

AMERICANIZATION FOR LOYALTY

AND PATRIOTISM, 1916-1930

★ ★ ★ ★ ★

Pupil Leader:	Salute the flag! [A salute is given followed by the Pledge of Allegiance]
Leader:	Why do we salute the flag?
Assembly:	Because we desire to honor it.
Leader:	Why should we honor it?
Assembly:	Because it stands for liberty, justice and equal opportunities in life for all those who live under its folds.
Leader:	How can we best show our devotion to the flag?
Assembly:	By obeying the laws of our country.
Leader:	Who are the enemies of the flag?
Assembly:	All persons who strike at our flag by war or who break the laws that have been made to keep our liberties.
Leader:	What are our duties as citizens?
Assembly:	First, always to defend the honor of our country; second, to obey the laws and see that others obey them; and third, always to remember that first of all we are American citizens, whose duty it is to stand by our country and keep its flag free from dishonor.[1]

Seattle school students often greeted their day with a flag salute much like the one above. A pupil leader, most often a boy, held the American flag in stalwart fashion while the rest of the student body, with their right arms extended outward, recited the assembly portion of the salute. Such flag rituals and various flag assemblies aimed to instill loyalty, citizenship, and respect for American ideals. They were critical components in the Americanization efforts for children of immigrant parents, ethnic minorities, and white, native students. This tradition in the Seattle Public Schools became a permanent fixture in the school day after the passage of a flag law in the fall of 1915.[2] In today's classrooms the recitation of the Pledge of Allegiance, albeit performed cursorily, is a vestige of the old flag rituals.

In this chapter I argue that Seattle had a tradition of steering a moderate course in response to Americanization pressures while stressing loyalty and Americanism. I examine curricular reforms, which placed heavy emphasis on the teaching of Western history, specialized programs for immigrant populations, and ongoing extracurricular activities to provide evidence for how the Seattle schools directed a moderate and progressive approach to Americanization and citizenship. Before those issues are examined in greater detail, I provide an overview of Seattle's demographics as well as a summary of national Americanization efforts.

From 1916 to 1930 the Seattle schools had at their core a philosophy of loyalty and patriotism in their approach to democratic citizenship education, with particular emphasis on the teaching of history. The thrust of Americanization nationwide contained seven different strands at the time: flag rituals; segregation in English language education; social welfare; thrift; citizenship curriculum; extracurricular activities; and grades for citizenship. Seattle used a modified version of each.

Urban schools across the United States represented a range in the type of Americanization programs offered. While others took the extreme in implementing English-only practices and denigrating their immigrant students to conform to Anglo standards, others offered more of a social welfare approach to the acculturation process. In Seattle, Superintendent Frank B. Cooper (1901–1922) early on resisted the efforts by Daughters of the American Revolution (DAR) and the Minute Men to control school curricula and activities devoted to patriotism and loyalty. Cooper also warned the Board of Directors against developing a permanent, segregated school for students with limited English proficiency. In his efforts to Americanize, Cooper stressed the importance of providing a curriculum relevant to the lives of students rather than emphasizing rote learning. Serving the needs of the community, the schools also offered night classes to adults, especially immigrant mothers, to learn the English language. All of these curricular and extracurricular components embodied the teaching of Americanization and citizenship in the Seattle schools from 1916 to 1930.

From the time of World War I up to the Great Depression, the Seattle schools' program on citizenship training comprised flag rituals and obeisance and reverence for laws. Patriotic ideals were a major focus in curricular and extracurricular activities. Nationwide, Americanization programs reached their zenith during the mass influx of immigration from southern and eastern Europe to urban areas in the United States. In a broad sense "Americanization," or the instilling of a "common culture," had always been a function of public schools.[3] During World War I, however, explicit Americanization programs, with an emphasis on loyalty and patriotism, as well as acculturation, became prevalent in U.S. schools. Partly as a means of social control *and* as a genuine way to respond to growing social crises, educators sought out policies and programs for acculturation and assimilation.

SEATTLE'S RACIAL DEMOGRAPHICS

Much literature on the history of racial minorities tends to focus on matters of "black and white," with specific references to the South, Midwest, and East Coast of the United States. The West Coast has always been multicultural, including Anglo, Mexican, American Indian, Asian, and African American populations.[4] Other regions in the United States also existed in complex multiracial relationships, but they did not have as many Asian residents as did the West Coast. Seattle, and much of the West Coast, had a very different immigrant and ethnic minority population than did cities on the East

Coast and in the Midwest. The distinctiveness of Seattle also lay in its Asian population's differing from those of Los Angeles and San Francisco. All these factors combined warrant a more critical look into how the Seattle schools reacted to a growing national challenge in educating its youth in the ideals of Americanism.

During the Progressive Era, Seattle and Los Angeles had the highest numbers of Japanese American residents in the United States.[5] The dominant nonwhite group (but not the dominant immigrant population) in Seattle between the turn of the century and World War II was Japanese Americans.[6] By 1940 Los Angeles County comprised more than 36,866 Japanese Americans; of these, almost two-thirds, or 23,321, lived in the city of Los Angeles.[7] Seattle came next, with almost 7,000 residents and another 2,700 in surrounding King County and 2,000 more in adjacent Pierce County.[8] Compared with the total population, the proportion of Japanese residents and Japanese Americans was higher in Seattle than in Los Angeles. Table 3.1 provides the population breakdown among the major minority groups in Los Angeles and Seattle in 1920.

While the numbers of Japanese and Chinese residents achieved relative parity in both cities, the differences in the populations of African Americans, Mexican Americans, and Filipinos are noteworthy. Los Angeles had a higher representation of African Americans and Mexicans, making up the majority of their minority population, whereas Seattle's Asian population, including Filipinos, constituted that city's majority racial ethnic mix. By 1910, Seattle's 6,127 Japanese were the fifth-largest ethnic group after the Canadians, Swedes, Norwegians, and Germans.[9] By 1916, ten churches, a variety of civic and social clubs, and five Japanese-language newspapers served Seattle's Japanese American community and areas beyond.[10]

Other urban areas across the nation recorded higher numbers and greater percentages of immigrants from northern and southern Europe. At the turn of the century, immigrants from Germany, Ireland, Italy, Poland, Hungary, and Czechoslovakia settled in New York, Ohio, Wisconsin, and

TABLE 3.1:
POPULATION OF LOS ANGELES AND SEATTLE'S MINORITY POPULATION IN 1920

1920 Los Angeles			1920 Seattle		
Group	Number	%	Group	Number	%
Japanese	8,536	1.5	Japanese	7,874	2.5
Chinese	2,062	0.4	Chinese	1,351	0.4
African Am.	15,579	2.7	African Am.	2,894	0.9
Mexicans	21,598	3.8	Filipino	458	0.1
LA Total	576,673	100.0	Seattle Total	315,312	100.0

Source: Judith Rosenberg Raftery, *Land of Fair Promise: Politics and Reform in Los Angeles Schools, 1885–1941* (Stanford: Stanford University Press, 1992), 12, 70, 102; and Quintard Taylor, *The Forging of a Black Community: Seattle's Central District from 1870 through the Civil Rights Era* (Seattle: University of Washington Press, 1994), 108.

Missouri.[11] The number of Asian immigrants never reached the levels evident in Los Angeles and Seattle. By 1940 the only sizable Japanese American community on the East Coast was in New York, where some twenty-five hundred lived.[12] In Chicago prior to World War II, only four hundred Japanese Americans lived in the city. During the war, however, Chicago replaced the West Coast as the center of Japanese American life in the United States.[13]

AMERICANIZATION AND CITIZENSHIP
IN THE SEATTLE PUBLIC SCHOOLS: 1916–1930

In the Seattle schools, the twinned ideas of loyalty and Americanism framed curricular and extracurricular instruction in citizenship. In terms of curriculum, an emphasis on the teaching of ancient Western civilization and training in thrift predominated for decades. English language instruction for adults in night schools, and for schoolchildren, through the Pacific School, were programmatic additions aimed at serving immigrant populations in various communities of Seattle. School assemblies, flag rituals, and citizenship clubs for boys and girls were also ongoing in-school and extracurricular activities for character building.

Flag rituals were to be held in all public gatherings in Washington State, including schools, starting in the fall of 1916. This statewide flag law of 1915 brought about its own set of tensions and conflicts between Superintendent Cooper and some of the community members in Seattle. The following excerpt of a memorandum by Frank Cooper to Josephine Preston, the state superintendent for public instruction, on February 18, 1916 illustrates the conflict and Cooper's response to nativist pressures:

> Last fall, soon after the opening of school, the attention of the principals was called to this newly enacted law regarding flag exercises and they were instructed to carry into effect the letter and spirit of the law as nearly as practicable. The particular method of doing this was left to them.

I believe that principals and teachers generally are in sympathy with the intention of this law. The fact that there has been used in this city for six or eight years past a flag ritual, a copy of which I am sending you, is evidence that we have not been unmindful of the desirability of improving citizenship through respect for the flag and what it stands for. I mention this as proof that I and those associated with me are not open to the charge of lightly regarding the inculcation of patriotic principles and sentiments, since we attended to such instruction before it became a matter of law.

I very much fear that a strict observance of this law, to hold flag exercises in every school every week, will defeat the purpose of the law and its authors. I think the attention of the Daughters of the American Revolution should be called to the fact that there are certain psychological effects unfavorable to accomplishment of the desired end which may have been overlooked in enthusiasm for the end to be achieved. I wonder as to the effect upon high school boys and girls of having them participate every week in flag exercises and a flag salute according to the prescribed legal formula laid down. I think that it would be easy for those who are conversant with the reactions of boys and girls in the adolescent period to conceive how a distaste for flag exercises and for the flag itself might result in the minds of many from the weekly repetition of this formal exercise. With the smaller children this would not be true, but I think it would be much better even there to leave to the patriotic initiative of the teacher the selection of time and occasion. In this way what would be a stimulating and inspiring exercise would not become perfunctory and tasteless. If this law is strictly observed, a pupil in his course through the grades and high school will have participated in this formal exercise every week of every year through his entire course. Is it not possible that we may do more harm to the patriotic impulse and to the inspired feeling which should accompany the sight of "Old Glory" by a strict observance of this law than if its purpose were carried out with less attention to regularity and to formality?

I wish you might suggest to the ladies of the D.A.R. the advisability of securing the opinions of high school principals and grade principals, also, regarding the possible effects as to the literal carrying out of this law. I may be wrong. If I am, I am willing to be put right.[14]

Cooper's expression of his professional and personal distaste for a structured and formalized flag ritual was representative of his administrative style as superintendent. He argued for symbolic flag rituals emphasizing lessons on the meaning behind the flag over rote exercises. Cooper saw teachers and principals as competent professionals in developing and implementing appropriate loyalty and patriotic programs for their students. This is illustrative of the kinds of political pressures in which Cooper was embroiled with the conservative civic organizations in Seattle.

Frank Cooper, well known for his progressive education measures, found himself entangled in ideological battles with staunch traditionalists throughout his tenure. His response to the members of the Daughters of the American Revolution set the stage for how the Seattle Public Schools would approach citizenship education and Americanization beyond his term as superintendent. While understanding the need to appease, to a degree, the demands of patriotic organizations, Cooper, nevertheless, voiced his opinions where he felt it mattered.

Under Cooper's leadership flag exercises and districtwide curricular attention to civic ideals, primarily through the teaching of history, remained. Even after Cooper's resignation in 1922, the Seattle schools steered a moderate course of Americanization. Curricular content as well as extracurricular activities, in-school exercises, and night classes constituted the major efforts by the Seattle schools to Americanize its students and immigrant communities. The rest of the chapter describes how the Seattle schools framed their citizenship education programs, based on the themes of loyalty and Americanism, through various curricular reforms, programmatic additions, and extracurricular activities from 1916 to 1930.

LOYALTY AND AMERICANISM: THE TWINNED GOALS

Loyalty. Loyalty framed one purpose of curricular and extracurricular activities of the Seattle Public Schools' teachings on citizenship and Americanization from 1915 to 1942. The thrust of this effort came from nationalis-

tic sentiments during World War I and state legislation making flag ceremonies mandatory at all public gatherings in Seattle and other cities after its
passage in 1915.[15] As discussed in the previous section, in schools the issue
over how the flag exercises should be implemented was a point of contention between the DAR and Frank B. Cooper, superintendent of Seattle
Public Schools at the time. Cooper defended his position to allow for a loose
interpretation of the flag law. The intent of the law was to heighten loyalty
and improve "citizenship through respect for the flag and what it stands
for."[16]

Cooper's desire was to uphold the spirit of the law and to allow individual school principals and teachers to implement the program as they saw fit.
He pointed out that a literal translation of the flag law would essentially be
"perfunctory and tasteless."[17] As in the case of other urban areas across the
United States, the Daughters of the American Revolution and other civic
organizations sought influence in matters of patriotism in the schools. The
era of "political fundamentalism" and formalized Americanization efforts in
schools magnified.

Compulsory Americanization did not reach its peak until the decade
after World War I. David Tyack and James Thomas refer to this period as
"political fundamentalism in education," for many patriotic, civic, and legal
organizations such as the American Legion, the Grand Army of the Republic, the American Bar Association, Daughters of the American Revolution,
the National Security League, the Constitution Anniversary Association,
and the Better America Federation worked to secure orthodox political
instruction.[18] By 1923 an overwhelming percentage of states subscribed to
patriotic instruction or rituals in the following areas: history of the United
States (90 percent), citizenship (81), flag displays (81), and all instruction in
English (73), among others.[19] This structure of mandated public programs
embraced a range of policies and attitudes toward immigrants and Americanization that prevailed within and among different districts.

Superintendent Cooper's and the DAR's dispute over the flag law was
indicative of efforts by various civic and community groups to assert their

influence over school policies. In the spring of 1916, there was much pressure on the schools to allow for military training as a program in war preparation.[20] Despite opposition and resistance to military training by the Seattle schools, the state legislature placed compulsory military training in high schools in 1917.[21] War preparedness also centered on flag saluting as one its activities.

Further, volunteer nativist groups, such as the Minute Men, exerted their own brand of patriotism by seeking to influence and control how schools functioned during the First World War. Historian Bryce Nelson highlights four ways in which the Minute Men sought to change school activities:

> First, they were often involved in successful attempts to fire teachers who were unsupportive of the war. Second, they were prominent in the recall of board member Anna Louise Strong [a pacifist labor leader]. Third, they led the drive to drop German as an elective foreign language. And fourth, they led the drive to drop certain textbooks thought to be pro-German.[22]

In all matters having to do with the character of classroom instruction (as opposed to the character of school board politics), Superintendent Cooper resisted the efforts of nativist groups. However, his judgments were eventually overruled by a more conservative board, and he himself was forced to resign in 1922 over some of these very issues. Outside group influences, especially during 1916–1921, became one of many tensions the Seattle Public Schools faced in the implementation of various Americaniza-tion programs.

CURRICULAR REFORMS FOR CITIZENSHIP
AND AMERICANIZATION

Americanism through History and Civics. The Seattle Public Schools articulated a philosophy of Americanism that served as the foundation for the principles and ideals of a civic life: "Americanism is more than a system of government; it is the spirit of a national life. The American people believe in self-government tempered with wisdom. They believe also that a nation has a right to live its own life without interference by other nations."[23] This definition given by the Seattle schools in 1916 was one of the guiding principles upon which to enact school curricula toward the goal of living in a democracy. Such a concept underlay how students in the first grade through high school would be taught patriotism and ideals of American citizenship. The schools were to emphasize this as practice and theory in all their grades.

Nationally, concepts of Americanism contained different definitions and purposes. The following excerpt from a national 1920 *Handbook Series on Americanization* provides another perspective in understanding how Americanism was viewed by educators all across the United States at the time. In this particular view, Americanism was seen as

> a matter of spirit, to be regarded and approached in a spirit of truth. It breaks down race and class prejudice...Americanism makes democracy possible...As Americans if we could but grasp the elementary fact that Americanism is always partial and incomplete, an ideal to be sought but never fully to be attained because always in its perfection just beyond our reach, how much better Americans might we ourselves become, and how far more potent missioners of the gospel of Americanism would be.[24]

This view of Americanism contained a humanistic principle, of breaking down the barriers of race and class differences, and a social gospel message as a means for proselytizing foreigners toward the common good of American ideals, including an inculcation into Protestant ideology.

In a more extreme fashion, Superintendent William Wirt of the Gary schools in Indiana incorporated religious study into the school curriculum. Part of the Americanization process, in Wirt's conception, necessarily included instruction, and conversion, to (Protestant) religious ideals.[25] Although the Seattle schools did not go to such measures in enforcing

Protestant ideals, the Jewish community leaders of Seattle, and in other urban areas, saw public schools as a negative influence in this regard. Some within the Seattle chapter of the Council of Jewish Women feared that public school teachers and administrators acted too much as Christianizing agents to newly arrived Jewish immigrants. As a result a number of the educational programs devised by the Jewish settlement workers counteracted the Protestant-based aims within the Seattle Public Schools' Americanization efforts.[26]

In the Seattle Public Schools, the Americanization curriculum, with a concentration on loyalty and Americanism, followed a general, three-part outline published in the *Quinquennial Report* of 1921. The report emphasized lessons in civics and history for the high school level. Part one emphasized an understanding of "The Great War" and the various motives and decisions of the respective countries in their quest for peace. This format aimed to help students comprehend why wars developed and consider the "real" motives of each country in their involvement in World War I. Determining the "real" motives was to be left open for classroom discussion.

Part two examined the progress of democracy through a strong emphasis on ancient Greek history. The connection to democratic civilizations of the past and the lessons to be learned from that knowledge was the intent of the lessons drawn from Greek history. According to the Seattle Public Schools' report:

> American history and civics, building on the foundation thus laid, teach the duties and responsibilities of every intelligent patriotic citizen, 'To be honest and upright; to obey the law; to assist in law enforcement; to seek no special privilege; to vote for upright and competent citizens; to insist on protection and justice for all; to respect the flag as the symbol of his country; to recognize that national need comes before private case and comfort, and the salvation of his country before his own life.'[27]

An intelligent citizen was one who embodied loyalty and patriotism with a concern for communitarian goals. An understanding of the importance of the collective need over one's individual needs was a focus of history and civics. This explanation, of a civics curriculum moving away from individualism and independence, was part of a dramatic and radical move away from the "old" civics to the "new."[28] In 1915 the National Education Association endorsed a new civics curriculum that ignored formal politics and government in favor of cooperation and community.[29] Citizenship moved away from political rights and voting toward a cultural ideal and identity. An examination of *The Seattle Educational Bulletin*, a monthly district newsletter for administrators, teachers, and community members, from 1920 to 1942 revealed a significant number of reports on the current trends within the NEA. It is not surprising, then, that the Seattle schools were influenced by national curricular reforms.

Part three examined various social and economic problems such as the "agrarian question, the colonial policy, the alien problems, the organization of industry, and the development of social life."[30] This was designed to address the political issues and challenges to the development of a democracy. Again, the specific details of these issues were to be discussed in individual classrooms.

In the Seattle Public Schools from 1921 to 1924, history and civics lessons were central and ongoing components of citizenship education. In the *Triennial Report* of 1924, curricular attention to American civic ideals and patriotism was emphasized for the first eight grades. High school students could not graduate without passing requisite courses in history and civics. Thus for all grades, a heavy stress on lessons in American history dominated. The typical history lesson would focus on the "heroes" of American society and how, through their stories, one would learn about "the struggles of the early patriots against a despotic king, the winning of the West, the liberation of the slaves, and other high lights of American history. . . ."[31] The focus of such curriculum reform centered on perpetuating the European-American norm of Western civilization and democracy. Such inculcation of patriotic sentiments, continuing its way through high schools, was to contribute "directly to citizenship training by education for thoughtful participation in government based upon true American ideals."[32] Documentation of patriotic activities, led by educational specialists, was soon adopted by schools to measure the time expended for particular activities.

Efforts to carefully gauge and measure the time spent on various classroom instruction came from the Department of Research, established in October of 1922 with Dr. Fred C. Ayers as the director. Ayers was responsible for studying the educational problems connected with the administration of the curriculum, instruction, supervision, and the progress of the pupils.[33] Included in the *Triennial Report* of 1921–1924 was a detailed account of the number of minutes the Seattle schools expended on core subject areas (reading, arithmetic, history, science, civics, etc.) and other programs (drawing, supervised play, recess, arts, etc.) in comparison to the national average. Seattle led the nation's average when it came to reading (2,567 minutes a week versus 2,003), history (900 versus 616), and supervised play (650 versus 136).[34] This finding indicates the degree to which the Seattle schools emphasized the importance of history instruction in teaching American civic ideals. It is also apparent how scientific management of schools in the Progressive Era led to such detailed accounting of minutes spent on classroom instruction of all subject areas.

The teaching of history and civics was again stressed in the 1924–1927 *Triennial Report* for training in patriotism and service. A 1925 study revealed that the Seattle schools devoted an average of 51 percent more time to American history and civics than the rest of the nation's schools.[35] The study of the Constitution and its link to liberty and democracy in the development of the United States as a "great world power" provided training for the young citizen. The justification for such an emphasis was "primarily to utilize the impressionable years, which are those of the elementary school, for the inculcation of patriotic sentiments and ideals."[36]

An assessment of how students learned and practiced "good citizenship" was done through the grading of qualities to facilitate proper behavior. Students' citizenship was graded on the points of: courtesy, promptness, dependability, cheerful cooperation, self-reliance, initiative, thrift, self-control, good sportsmanship, school service, and good workmanship.[37] Such itemization of ideal modes of behavior for good citizenship was meant to aid parents in teaching proper behavior at home. In this manner, a close coordination between school and home life would provide a consistent and continuous link in the Americanization effort.

Training in Thrift. The thrift component of the regular "course of study in citizenship" grew from the schools' sale of thrift stamps and liberty bonds as a part of their service during World War I. Under Superintendent Thomas R. Cole, a school savings plan was adopted on March 13, 1923 and put into operation in all elementary and high schools.[38] The feature of the school savings plan called for weekly "bank days" for pupils to make deposits. The emphasis lay more on learning the habit of saving, rather than on the amount deposited: the act of saving would build character, deemed an "American" virtue. The savings plan was a voluntary effort by the students, and by the district's account most schools were reporting anywhere from 70 to 100 percent of the student body making deposits.[39] Another lesson school personnel hoped students would learn from the savings plan was that upon leaving high school, graduates would know how to earn, save, and invest money, thereby contributing to the economic revitalization of their community. A thrift committee developed by Superintendent Cole reported on the progress of the school savings plan and indicated that students learned the value of money and began to budget whatever small incomes they had.[40]

In Los Angeles, school savings banks were introduced as early as 1900, and by the time the Depression hit, many bankers felt that the savings concept needed reinforcing.[41] The Americanizers of Los Angeles felt that "given the opportunity and intelligent guidance," immigrants could "best Americanize themselves when left to their own devices and to the skills and ingenuity of the native leaders."[42] One such service offered by the schools was the opening and maintaining of savings accounts by children. A good citizen, developed through particular habits of character education, was essentially made and not born.

Extensions of Citizenship Education. An extension of citizenship was slowly broadened, in terms of curriculum, to the study of the natural environment and health and hygiene as highlighted in the 1927–1930 *Triennial Report.* Americanism ideals, such as loyalty and patriotism, served secondary purposes to an exploration of the environment and nature, increased attention to handwriting standards through penmanship tests, and basic application of health principles.

According to the *Report*, natural science education underwent reform, particularly for the elementary grades, from 1928 to 1930. The University of Washington and Seattle's Audubon Society led the efforts to provide teacher training in plant sciences and courses in bird study, respectively. In justifying the move toward a more experiential curriculum, the *Report* states, "[T]eachers recognized the value of a knowledge of the out-of-doors as a joy to be experienced by the children; as an aid in appreciation of our great wealth of natural and scenic beauties; as a basis for teaching some phases of the social subjects; and as a general aid to good citizenship through a knowledge of practical conservation."[43]

The study of natural science in the Seattle schools was formalized in 1929 with thirty-one platoon schools offering such courses, either alone or in combination with art, penmanship, or hygiene.[44] Adopting the innovative measure begun by William Wirt of the Gary schools in Indiana, Seattle followed suit with their version of the platoon system. The marriage of science with art, penmanship, and hygiene instruction is an odd relationship, to be sure, but a connecting thread of orderliness, regimentation, and (bodily) control is evident throughout.

Penmanship tests became a regular feature for elementary school children at the time. They were judged by the standards deemed appropriate for their grade level, and efforts were under way to compare the test results of Seattle's schoolchildren with others around the nation. Students were encouraged to develop the habit of self-criticism by frequent comparisons with the standard of their grade.[45] The students were forced, to a large degree, to mind their p's and q's.

With the appointment of a Seattle schoolteacher to a national committee on health education in Washington, D. C., physical education and health and hygiene matters received a greater degree of attention in the *Report*. The reform measure for physical education in elementary schools provided for the segregation of boys and girls with "appropriate" programs planned to fit their specific needs. A program for girls in platoon schools, "Natural Expression through Rhythm," included exercises for body control, folk dancing, and the interpretation of nature, music, literature, and art through rhythmic movements.[46] Again, intimated in the description of the course is the language of control, regimentation, and self-regulation of one's body.

Another aspect of such attention to bodily matters came in the form of hygiene, health and cleanliness inspection, and weighing and measuring. Such daily rituals also became normative practice of school life in Gary, Indiana. William Wirt felt that attention to cleanliness and hygiene was especially important for immigrant children, as he believed them to be the most lacking in such areas.[47] For Wirt, and for many progressive reformers, Americanization embodied an internalization of health and hygiene practices. For the same reason and/or in response to growing cases of contagious diseases, especially in overcrowded urban areas, Seattle school officials employed a limited number of nurses to treat children who teachers felt required more careful screening.

Consequently, concern for underweight children in the Seattle schools gave rise to the weighing and measuring of students twice a year, in October and March, beginning in 1925.[48] According to the schools' figures, school life was favorable to weight gain; whereas summer vacations, with irregular sleeping and eating habits, tended to result in a loss of weight for many children. The report by health professionals indicated that such attention to hygienic habits of living helped children put on weight. Certainly, with the Depression under way at this time, the stress on health habits, cleanliness, and weight gain is understandable. Curriculum reform was designed to meet the real-life needs of many students.

"English for Foreigners." The Seattle schools developed services specific to immigrant populations at the same time they reconfigured their approaches to history and civics lessons. Americanization classes for adults, aimed specifically at foreign mothers of immigrant schoolchildren, became a primary additive feature. Superintendent Cooper proposed to establish English classes for foreign mothers so that the ideals of Americanism would flow down to subsequent generations. Cooper explained:

> As part of one general scheme for the promotion of good citizenship and sound Americanism we shall begin this year along with our regular program of instruction of children in the principles and practice of the civic virtues, with the awakening of a sense of obligation among the children of non-English speaking parents to encourage their parents to learn our national language and to become interested in and acquainted with American ideals and institutions. This, in order that a better and safer national heritage may be left to the children for whom our foreign born parents are making a home. Any really effective scheme of Americanisation must include reaching the home of foreign people using a language other than English, in our community, and one influential means of reaching such homes is by way of the mothers and through the cooperation of the children attending American schools from those homes.[49]

Reflecting much of the Progressive Era rhetoric on acculturation of immigrant children, Cooper saw mothers as central figures in the home for successful Americanization. Mothers, then, would take on the moral responsibility of raising civic-minded individuals at home, with teachers and administrators filling the gap at school. The historian George Sánchez's use of the popular slogan for Americanization in the Los Angeles area for Mexican immigrants, "Go after the women," is a befitting phrase for Cooper's attempts to reach the mothers.[50] The revitalization of republican motherhood was under way. The schools' efforts to lessen the cognitive dissonance some students might feel between home and school would supposedly be addressed through contiguous means to promote the speaking of English. In some ways Seattle's program for teaching English to immigrant mothers was similar to the work of progressive social reformers in Los Angeles through an Americanization program enacted in 1915.

The Home Teacher Act (HTA) of 1915 was a specific Americanization program in Los Angles targeting immigrant women, mothers who normally did not seek English or naturalization classes elsewhere.[51] A notable aspect of this act was that certified teachers, trained in specific courses, were responsible for teaching immigrant women, in addition to being employed at a regular elementary school. The social welfare model as approached in the HTA primarily serviced the needs of immigrant Mexican women. The reformers involved in the HTA were concerned with studying nutritional deficiencies, providing basic medical attention, and acting as liaisons between immigrant families and social service agencies. Although a large number of Mexican families adopted particular measures enacted by the HTA, Americanization efforts largely failed when confronted with the fundamental cultural practices of Mexican immigrant families. According to Sánchez two principal reasons underlay the failure of the program: (1) Mexican immigrants in the 1920s never fully committed themselves to integration into American life. (2) The various forces behind Americanization programs never assembled an optimistic ideological approach that might have attracted Mexican immigrant women.[52] This failure is an indication of how Mexican immigrants' sense of cultural agency and self-determination became a mode of resistance to a European-American model of Americanization.

A closer resemblance to the HTA in Seattle came in the form of the settlement work provided by the Council of Jewish Women (CJW), separate from the efforts enacted by the Seattle Public Schools. The CJW was responsible for administering social service programs targeting Jewish immigrants in the Central area of Seattle. The first settlement home, opened on April 12, 1906 on Washington and Twelfth South, emphasized religious, philanthropic, and educational purposes. It was designed strictly to be a "social center"—a bureau of observation.[53] The first night school for foreigners was established in November 1909 for English language and citizenship. It met two nights a week, and the participants included Jewish women and men, among them Greeks, Italians, and other nationalities with a total number of attendees between forty and fifty.[54] According to a report in 1913, the principal departments were sewing and Sabbath school—as a number of members felt that the public schools offered a Protestant-based education for their children. The dedication of the permanent Settlement House at 304 eighteenth South and Main took place on December 29, 1916. The CJW's Settlement House remained a strong community feature well into the Second World War.

Although the Seattle schools did not offer an extensive social welfare model like the HTA of Los Angeles or the CJW's Settlement House, it did provide Americanization classes as part of the evening school curricula. The courses offered were: (1) English for foreigners; (2) American history, civics, geography, and literature; and (3) Naturalization classes for men and women who wished to get their final citizenship papers.[55] By 1921 the Seattle schools offered Americanization classes (twelve months in the year) for those wishing to attain citizenship and for foreign-born mothers who desired to learn English and to know American customs.[56] The American customs foreign mothers became acquainted with were those closely tied to domesticity. Many children of the mothers who attended Americanization classes most likely attended Pacific School, a transition school for students learning English as a second language, at some point in their schooling.

The Pacific School. The Pacific School, situated at 510 Eleventh Avenue in Seattle's Capitol Hill neighborhood, served as a transition school for students with limited English proficiency. It was a school of "distinct classes for newly arrived young foreigners who sought admission to the day classes."[57] Four classrooms were designated specifically for the teaching of English language to "foreigners." Students above the primary grades who were not fluent in English attended Pacific until they were able to gain proficiency and comprehension in English. Once students reached a level of fluency, they were admitted into their "regular day schools."

A description of the Pacific School and of the general structure of its curriculum and program follows:

> The Japanese form the largest group; the Chinese the second; the Russians the third in point of number; with individuals from many European countries. These pupils are not classified according to their knowledge of English for they have too little of that for examinations or tests of any kind. All these factors are considered briefly. An interpreter is called in and some idea is obtained of the applicant's education and intelligence and he is assigned to the group which promises to contribute most for his immediate inspiration to hear and to speak English.
>
> Through these classes the foreign pupils are saved from embarrassment and discouragement and are helped by intensive training to overcome mannerisms and accents that otherwise persist through adult life.... Return to regular classes is conditioned upon their being able to use the English language reasonably well for the grade assigned.[58]

The Pacific school had been in existence since 1909, but it was not until the *Triennial Report* of 1924 that attention was paid to the specialized service offered by the school. By 1920, with the rising number of Asian American students, the Board of Directors requested Superintendent Cooper to submit the numbers of "Asiatic pupils" in the Seattle schools. The headcount recorded a total of 930 Asian students, with 704 Japanese (76 percent), 166 Chinese (17 percent), 65 Filipinos, 3 Armenians, 1 Korean, and 1 Russian.[59] Two years later, the Board of Directors requested Cooper to submit another report on the nationalities of students at the Pacific School, where Asian students predominated. It is important to note that not all students of the Pacific School required training in the English language. Students from the community, regardless of their fluency in English, attended Pacific, as did students in other areas and neighborhoods of Seattle. Table 3.2 reflects the total number of students attending Pacific School in 1922. Of the twenty-six different nationalities represented at the Pacific School, 269 students were born in the United States of immigrant parents—figures that would include the Nisei student population. Also, 96 of the 636 students at the Pacific School were enrolled in classes for "newly arrived foreign youth." The ethnic backgrounds of the 96 students were as follows: Japanese, 38; Chinese, 14; Russian Jews, 11; Turkish Jews, 22; Italian, 7; Swedish, 1; Latvians, 2; Greeks, 1.[60]

Students at the Pacific School represented an amalgamation of cultures. The area in which the school was located contained a high number of immigrants, Jews, and longtime residents of Seattle from various European countries. It is highly unlikely that students from Canada, England, and other parts of the United States required instruction in English. It is more the case that their families settled in the area around the Pacific School, as only 12 percent of the students lived outside of the school's district.[61]

The specialized service at the Pacific School gradually aimed to return all students into the "regular" day classes. There was a discussion, however, as to whether a permanent building should be allocated for segregated instruction for foreign students. Cooper expressed his disagreement with the proposal by the Board of Directors to consider a permanent, segregated building. He felt that the idea, if implemented, would be disadvantageous, both from an educational and a financial point of view and that an "arbitrary segregation would invite serious embarrassment and complications."[62] He argued that an immersion into American culture and ideals would provide for faster acculturation than confining foreign students to one building. Cooper advocated, instead, a process of transitioning students into regular day schools as swiftly as the students' skills warranted.

This middle course pursued by Superintendent Cooper contrasts with the most virulent English-only efforts in specific areas of the United States.

TABLE 3.2:
NATIONALITIES OF STUDENTS AT PACIFIC SCHOOL
IN 1922

Nationalities of Students at Pacific School	Number
Japanese	156
Chinese	35
Jewish [Polish (9), Russian (37), Spanish (38), Turkish (78), Austrian (2)]	164
Italian	18
Greek	3
Finnish	16
Danish	3
Norwegian	7
Swedish	11
French	2
South American	1
Belgian	3
Latvian	2
German	4
Austrian	1
English	16
Irish	3
Scotch	7
Welsh	1
Canadian	10
Eskimo/Inuit	1
African	17
U.S. American (ethnicity unknown)	153
TOTAL	636

Source: Adapted from: F. B. Cooper to BOD, 13 January 1922.

Although not yet a state, the territory of Hawaii was also affected by efforts at Americanizing its youth. Eileen Tamura's study "The English-Only Effort, the Anti-Japanese Campaign, and Language Acquisition in the Education of Japanese Americans in Hawaii, 1915–1940" examines the extent to which the English-only effort really dealt with language. Tamura's assertion is that it was really an anti-Japanese drive, targeting the Japanese language and the Nisei while disregarding other non-English languages and the children of other immigrants.[63]

In 1924 Hawaii began designating a set of schools as "English Standard."[64] A small group of Hawaiian residents sought to instill a WASP ideal of Americanism and Americanization. Following upon tumultuous past conflicts between Japanese American and Caucasian community leaders over the schooling of their youth, the English Standard movement encountered similar problems. For twenty-five years the English Standard schools, located mostly in Honolulu, were developed primarily for European American schoolchildren so that they would not be negatively influenced by Hawaiian Creole English and other forms of "non-Standard" English. Supporters of the cause argued that the schools would promote "Americanism by protecting the English language and encouraging good speech habits."[65] Critics called the Standard schools un-American due to discriminatory methods that encouraged race prejudice and marked a backward turn in the process of acculturation.[66] The emphasis lay in keeping white students from being "contaminated" by the "ways of the natives." Despite the generation of a fair amount of dispute, the Standard Schools were not phased out until 1949, when more middle-class Asians were able to effect change at the legislative level.[67]

The push toward "English-only" was not confined to Hawaii. The development of English Standard schools in Hawaii is a variant of the mainland phenomenon of laws against schools that taught non-English languages.[68] This is further evidence that Seattle again directed a moderate approach in educating immigrant students in English language instruction. While the Board of Directors of the Seattle Public Schools considered the possibility of establishing a permanent building for its foreign students, Frank Cooper was adamant in maintaining the course of transitioning students into their regular neighborhood schools.

ONGOING EXTRACURRICULAR ACTIVITIES AND IN-SCHOOL EXERCISES FOR CHARACTER BUILDING

School / Flag Assemblies as a Means of Citizenship Training. Weekly assemblies in the schools were seen as a way to foster ideals of citizenship. It was another ongoing component of the Seattle schools' education for loyalty and Americanism. Most Seattle schools held an assembly once a week by reciting a flag salute and giving the pledge of allegiance. Through the 1940s, it was commonplace for schools to participate in a flag ritual. Often used as a symbol to promote the ideals of Americanism and the "American dream," the flag salute would begin most school mornings. It had been a rare activity prior to World War I, but the United States' involvement in the war changed all that. The Seattle School Board placed American flags in classrooms, and flag-saluting exercises, much like the one described at the beginning of this chapter, became common.[69]

The approach to this particular form of Americanization rested on having students understand the flag as a symbol of civic ideals and patriotic loyalty. Flag ceremonies were justified as instilling a sense of duty to country,[70] as training for immediate and prospective citizenship as a member of a community, and as increasing pride in the students' schools. School administrators believed that these participatory efforts would overcome narrowness in character by developing intelligent citizens through daily recitations.[71] Again, the stress on an intelligent citizenry characterized by loyalty, patriotism, and an unquestioning faith in Americanism was the benchmark for the teaching of democracy at this time.

The use of school assemblies also gained in popularity throughout the nation as growing interest in raising the civic consciousness of students became the vogue. With citizenship in schools tied to student conduct and behavior, assemblies were seen as a way of promoting pride in schools, elevating citizenship, and increasing adherence to school laws and regulations.[72] Controlled activities, to foster the development of character, were also a response by educators to loosen the influence of modernism's grip on the youth of America. Industrialism and urbanization posed a threat to the development of communal values, and educators sought to elevate modes of effective individualism versus possessive individualism.[73]

PUPIL PARTICIPATION IN SCHOOL GOVERNMENT
AND HABIT TRAINING THROUGH CITIZENSHIP CLUBS

Extracurricular activities through Good Citizenship Clubs, Boys' Clubs, and Girls' Clubs were additional means of promoting Americanization. The aim here concentrated on developing the democratic character. One of the foundational conditions of these clubs required that students abide by a code of conduct that promoted values of being a "good citizen"; the emphasis, again, focused on one's behavior. School personnel often encouraged students to join such civic clubs and their activities. Certain schools had a "standards committee" that considered ways and means for establishing standards of conduct. An example is a code of conduct for girls in the Girls' Clubs:

MY CREED

I believe, as a High School girl of Seattle, I should be

Joyous, courageous and courteous.

Truthful, considerate and just.

Loyal and sincere in friendship.

Too noble to speak ill of others.

Willing to forgive and forget.

Prompt and gracious in obedience.

Ready to do all possible service.

Quick to appreciate what is done for me.

Respectful to my elders.

> True to the best that is within me that
> I may become a fine and worthy woman.[74]

The activities of the Boys' Club primarily concerned athletic competition in various sports, whereas the Girls' Club members gathered over committee matters in the vocational, social service, standards, extension, and health areas. While common virtues for character and moral development existed for boys and girls, specific activities for older students were drawn along gender lines. Girls were imbued with the traditional domestic virtues of sexual purity, gentleness, and meekness, whereas the boys received preparation for the world of work and family life.[75] These goals worked in tandem to promote a unified vision of a citizenry.

The emphasis on community activities and work toward the common good is an extension of the idea emphasizing community civics in citizenship education from 1915. National educational leaders championed reforms in the civics curriculum that looked to how schools could best serve its communities. Arthur William Dunn, Henry Thurston, and John Dewey were national educational leaders who viewed schools as a community and education as a service to the larger community to which it belonged.[76] Seattle, in all its functions, modeled its approach to citizenship education after the progressive thinkers of the time.

SUMMARY AND CONCLUSION

In summary, the case for Seattle embodies a progressively moderate approach to Americanization, citizenship, and character education. Also, the official policy was many things, even in one district: it represented a range as well as change over time. With regard to difference, the official attitude was more pluralistic than the programs in different urban areas at the time. There was the mention of having critical understanding of differences through discussion, and schools as places for opening up of opportunities of all races and economic classes. Seattle steered a moderate course in the face of political pressures.

Within the range of programs in Seattle, the assessment of the primary documents reveals a common strand throughout the decades. The Seattle Public Schools' devotion to Americanism, Americanization, and citizenship training retained a consistent core through curriculum revision, programmatic additions, and extra- and noncurricular activities. History and civics instruction were important components in how teachers taught for citizenship. Increased immigration, the role of various civic organizations, and the social and political upheavals no doubt played centrally in the schools' desire to implement strategic plans for educating citizens for school and community life.

The extent to which the programs were inculcating a narrow brand of citizenship, or even one pernicious to certain immigrant groups, remains an open question. The brief analysis of programs nationwide indicates that for some ethnic groups, Americanization was a euphemism for racial discrimination policies. The Seattle perspective comes solely from an administrative point of view and lacks views from students and non-English-speaking parents. Superintendent Cooper's initial desire to celebrate a broad interpretation of the flag law perhaps set the tone for how Seattle would approach the national push for a limited view of Americanization and acculturation. Cooper, it seems, spent time addressing outside groups' interests on how the schools ought to operate in light of wartime events.

To be sure, the nation in general and Seattle in particular did partake of patriotic instructions or political fundamentalism as noted by the historians Tyack and Thomas. Popular programs consisted of studying a revised version of U.S. history, learning about citizenship, participating in flag exercises and displays, and emphasizing classroom learning of Standard English. The Seattle Public Schools enacted various forms of all these curricula.

The Seattle case is distinctive, not only because of the makeup of its nonwhite population but because of the ways in which various Americanization programs were set in place. Seattle did not support explicit policies of ethnic erasure as did the Gary Schools, a concerted English Standard movement such as in Hawaii's schools, or the social welfare movement backed by Los Angeles. The Seattle schools embraced both traditional and progressive approaches in the implementation of a moderate approach to Americanization.

Referring to the well-known labor radicalism that characterized Seattle during World War I, Roger Sale discusses Seattle as a city that somehow became a place of radical ideas at the same time as it experienced growing conservatism.[77] Undoubtedly, the Seattle schools were also places where radical and bourgeois ideals clashed and merged. It was not outside the realm of local and national politics; in fact, the schools were very much a reflection of local politics. Also important at this time were the demographic and social changes that took place in Seattle. Although Japanese Americans formed a large group of immigrants in Seattle, the total immigrant and non-white population did reach the kind of critical mass as in other, more established urban settings.

To be fair, the other urban cases were also reflective of their local demographic and political situations. Seattle was a much younger city,[78] in comparison with those of the East Coast and Midwest and with other West Coast cities, and it was still in the midst of developing a local politics of its own. Other urban areas across the United States already had strong, well-established political machines with control over public schools. Further, these areas had to contend with population influx long before the West Coast, and programs of Americanization, though not specifically so called, were implemented in those places. Also, the higher number of immigrant and minority groups in a concentrated, urban area may have contributed to some schools' more segregative approach to Americanization. Although Seattle's Japanese American population was the highest nonwhite population, it did not reach beyond 3 percent of the total population. Seattle was still overwhelmingly white, and minority groups did not constitute a numerically significant group prior to the Second World War.

Curriculum in citizenship education was also reformed in the 1930s to reflect a more cosmopolitan concept. The Great Depression, political unrest in Europe, racism in the United States and increased anti-Semitic activities at home and abroad necessitated a response by educators to provide relevant education for all students. The PEA, the NEA, and key actors in the Intercultural Education movement all played a hand in the national reform efforts. Seattle also joined in the efforts to promote a more intercultural education through tolerance and understanding in their schools. The next chapter examines how the Seattle Public Schools' approach to Americanization and citizenship evolved into a more inclusive framework in response to the Depression and the Second World War.

Chapter 4

AMERICANIZATION BROADENED:

EDUCATION FOR TOLERANCE

AND INTERCULTURALISM

★   ★   ★   ★   ★

The 1930s and the Great Depression, just prior to the Second World War, carried their own set of challenges for schools. One cannot overstate the severity of economic losses of businesses and families. Massive unemployment and subsequent migrations of families in search of work all interrupted the basic functions of schools. During this time, the growing racial crises and the rise of anti-Semitism abroad, with events such as *Kristallnacht*, compelled leaders in national educational organizations to reconceptualize notions of tolerance, religious freedom, and a democratic way of life. Character education became the focus for successful citizenship. The Seattle schools, through curricular and extracurricular content, also used similar concepts to educate its students on the values of civic ideals. Education for vocation no longer held appeal with the massive rise in unemployment during the Depression. Schools refocused their efforts toward a greater understanding of the democratic process and redoubled their efforts toward tolerance and interculturalism.

Ideas of "tolerance" and "intercultural education" were introduced in the official curricula guides of the Seattle Public Schools from the mid- to late 1930s and early 1940s. Although the specific terminology of interculturalism was not used in official documents until 1941, the main ideas promoted by intercultural educationists and the Progressive Education Association influenced Seattle's curriculum reform measures as early as 1935. Two main texts that served to promote progressive ideals and vision toward character education and the democratic way of life were *Successful Living*[1] and *Living Today—Learning for Tomorrow*. *Successful Living*, published in 1935, was a handbook to be used by all teachers in promoting good character, eventually leading to good citizenship practices. *Living Today— Learning for Tomorrow*, published in 1938, was a social studies curriculum guide for all grades. Subject areas in history, civics, geography, and the environment were outlined in a way to develop connections between the individual and society. During this time the language of citizenship gave way to character education and democracy. While one may argue that character and democracy are fundamental components of citizenship education, the schools' concentration and specific use of the words "character education" and "democracy" indicate a shift in the schools' thinking that broadened and deepened the concept of citizenship.

A more inclusive notion of citizenship derived from—among other reasons—the economic unrest of the 1930s. Seattle schools at this time were, like the rest of the nation, experiencing the effects of the Great Depression. Teachers' salary cuts and deep budget woes drastically curtailed many school activities. *The Bulletin* suspended publication from September 1932 to March 1934.[2] As in New York City, Seattle teachers were asked to "'donate' a part of their pay, their time, and their good-will."[3] Without a doubt, other district staff salaries and programs suffered from financial exigencies. It became more difficult to argue that a good education would lead to job security when even some school officials had difficulties earning a subsistence wage.

With regard to curriculum, Superintendent Worth McClure reportedly adopted a modified version of the "platoon system" in Seattle that had originated in Gary, Indiana, under Superintendent William A. Wirt.[4] The result amounted to limited specialization in the lower grades whereby the teachers were relieved of certain duties by having others teach music, physical education, and fine arts.[5] This may have been a way to offset teachers' having to "volunteer" one's salary.

THE PROGRESSIVE EDUCATION ASSOCIATION
AND INTERCULTURAL EDUCATION

The Progressive Education Association (PEA), founded by Stanwood Cobb in 1919, started out as an organization of parents and laypeople whose base was the elite private schools of the East, but the PEA reached mass appeal in the 1930s with a socially concerned leadership interested in the reform of public education.[6] Indeed, their initial goals aimed "at nothing short of reforming the entire school system of America."[7] While what exactly the organization wished to accomplish remained unclear—not unlike the debates centering on the meaning of progressive education, past and present—PEA managed to garner more than 10,000 members at its peak in 1930. Indeed, *Time* magazine's coverage of the organization in the 31 October 1938 issue marked genuine recognition of the PEA.[8]

The PEA's concern for race and ethnicity grew out of increasing social unrest in the 1930s. The organization and its leaders, such as Executive Secretary Frederick Redefer, urged a socially responsible agenda that looked at issues of race and ethnicity raised by scholars such as Charles Adamic.[9] The organization's journal, *Progressive Education*, beginning in 1935 published considerably on human relations, intercultural education, and the uses of materials on ethnicity in the classroom.[10]

The push for interculturalism was the brainchild of Rachel Davis Du Bois. She was the founder and first executive of the Service Bureau for Intercultural Education.[11] Her pacifism, Quaker roots, and past experiences of feeling like an outsider forged a strong belief in developing empathic understanding with immigrants and racial minorities. Du Bois's particular interest in the writings of W. E. B. Du Bois,[12] especially his remarks that wars were a consequence of intergroup hatred, helped her to formulate classroom teaching methods, as a high school social studies teacher, in connecting the idea of international peace and intergroup understanding through assembly programs:

> [I]t brought together the entire student body; permitted actual demonstrations of the artistic achievements of ethnic groups; provided a forum for visiting ethnic group leaders, and permitted an appeal to the students' emotions as well as their intellects, a feature of the program that Du Bois came to insist made it pedagogically superior to strictly intellectual approaches. With the assistance of a student-faculty committee, she planned a year-long series of assemblies, held at two to six week intervals, each devoted to history, achievements and contributions of a particular ethnic group.[13]

Du Bois's approach to arouse the sympathies of the young through assemblies was refined as a doctoral student at Teachers College, Columbia University. Her proximity to immigrant groups and racial minorities in New York City and her associations with progressive educators such as William Kilpatrick, George Counts, and Daniel Kulp II helped her to lay out a systematic program of understanding attitude formation and prejudices. Du Bois's work continued through the 1930s as her influence reached the leaders of the PEA. Through PEA sponsorship, the Service Bureau for Intercultural Education entered the mainstream of America's schools. As Du Bois's biographer asserts, from 1924 through the 1930s, she was probably the first American educator to develop ethnic studies curriculum materials for the public schools.[14]

Du Bois published a number of articles in *Progressive Education*. In a March 1935 issue titled "Our Enemy—The Stereotype," she wrote about how the "pictures in our minds" operate to render one ethnic group as somehow inherently different, and thus inferior, from the dominant group. Stereotypes are the measures by which American society has kept racial minorities at a cultural and economic disadvantage. She continued:

As long as we have economic competition, we of the dominant group are going to use stereotypes to justify our exploitation of another group which is "different." As long as we feel that we are "different," we cannot unite in one common effort to change the economic system. As long as the Jew is pictured as the crafty money-getter, anti-Semitism and pogroms remain possible even in the United States. As long as the Negro is considered to be "different," lynching will continue. As long as "foreign" is thought of as being synonymous with "inferior," America will be culturally poor.[15]

The responsibility of the schools, Du Bois asserted, lay in devising assembly programs offering opportunities for cultural exchange. An example of such a program would involve community leaders of different cultural groups coming to schools to give talks on how negative stereotypes affect their communities. In return, students would later engage in dramatic sketches illustrating how the "power of vicarious living through drama is used as a means of building further understanding."[16] She also urged teachers to move beyond parochialism by opening their social experiences to people outside their own race. Here Du Bois emphasized how teachers had a direct impact on the degree to which intercultural education succeeded or failed.

In terms of curricular reform, Du Bois felt that effective change was possible only through the introduction of selective materials of ethnic minority and immigrant groups, incorporating, for example, sections on racial histories and cultural achievements into the courses of study.[17] Her content analysis of texts at the time revealed an overwhelming amount of misinformation and misleading facts about Jews and African Americans, in particular: "Nothing of importance was found which would develop sympathetic attitudes toward our various culture groups. It was easier to count lines developing antagonisms. The proportion ran five hundred lines against the Negro, to fifty against the Jew and ten against the Southern European immigrant. . . . But no text mentions the fact that the first man to lose his life in the American Revolution was Crispus Attucks, a Negro."[18] Certainly, such lack of information required that teachers and other educators develop a more systematic way of gathering information on racial minorities. Du Bois was firm in her efforts, however, to preach the gospel of interculturalism.

The message of tolerance and interculturalism, however loosely interpreted by progressive educators, found its way to the administrators and school officials in Seattle. A survey of *The Bulletin* between 1925 and 1940 confirms a high degree of involvement between Seattle educators and national leaders within the National Education Association and the Progressive Education Association. Seattle was host to the annual NEA conference in July of 1927[19] and also hosted the regional conference of the PEA in 1934.[20] With close connections to the activities of the PEA, and subsequent reports of activities in *The Bulletin*, Seattle schools were influenced to varying degrees by the national movements in progressivism and intercultural education. The publication of *Successful Living* and of *Living Today— Learning for Tomorrow* was a project by a committee of Seattle educators dedicated to progressivism and tolerance.

SUCCESSFUL LIVING

The publication of *Successful Living* in 1935 aimed at implementing a cohesive set of ideals on citizenship, namely through character education. The authors of the guide, a committee of social studies and history teachers, emphasized progressive social goals through (1) character education and (2) integrating the idea of school as society. They examined how public schools, as laboratories of democracy, served to facilitate the process of living a democratic way of life. According to the authors, character education was to be thought of, "like health, as the productive way of living through which strength is acquired. Character education in America is the mastery of a truly democratic way of living...a way of living which conserves and produces as many values as possible for as many persons as possible over as long a time as possible. Character education is the facilitation of this way of life."[21] What the textbook authors hoped to accomplish was a more cohesive, coordinated approach emphasizing a progressive character education. At the time, the effects of the Depression and political unrest necessitated a broader understanding of how character was inextricably linked to citizenship.

In fashioning a progressive ideology—in its curricular and scientific management approaches to schooling—the committee of authors outlined eight major ideas that served as the basis for learning: Knowing and Doing, The "Either-Or" Fallacy, Opportunities in the Classroom, The Teacher as Counselor and Friend, School Life and Democratic Living, Play and Democratic Living, Changing Times and Ethical Principles, and Coordinating the Out-of-School Life.

1. Knowing and Doing addressed the tensions inherent in education between vocational efficiency and education for life—in the Deweyan sense of the word. As the Depression reconfigured many educators' thoughts on "why we educate," the appeal of a liberal arts education, with a concentration on the classics, surfaced once more. Hence the idea of education as "making a life" played centrally to the task of the development of character, especially since vocational work, or any work for that matter, was in limited supply.

2. The "Either-Or" Fallacy sought to draw connections from two seemingly oppositional ways of thinking: of how the everyday world of the classroom contributed to society's broader objective. It states that "No pupil can attain the highest mental development of which he is capable without establishing habits of accuracy, self-reliance, patience, and industry—essentials of good character."[22] It relied on efforts not to choose between a "classical" and a "vocational" education, but rather to interweave the two. The classroom would be the place where everyday habits of mind, character growth, would develop.

3. Opportunities in the Classroom were to be facilitated by the teacher in ensuring that all subject areas in the classroom connected, however obliquely, to the aims of character education. Mathematics, science, literature, history, and geography contained important markers for bridging the gap between subject area and citizenship.

4. The Teacher as Counselor and Friend expanded the role of teaching beyond pedagogical aims. The growth of specialized knowledge, administrative progressivism, and scientific management looked at particular ways of tending to the "problems of the child." Thus, teachers were responsible for monitoring a child's mental and physical deficiencies as such monitoring benefited the work of the Child Study Department.

5. School Life and Democratic Living attributed some of its ideas to John Dewey in that the school offered a place to equalize opportunities for all children. The committee saw that the school, "serving all the children of all people, has a unique opportunity for overcoming snobbery, reducing racial and class prejudices, and teaching the brotherhood of man."[23] Furthermore, "The individual must gain a consciousness of his civic responsibilities. Dewey reminds us of the fact that school is not only a preparation for life; it is life itself. It may be so organized as to afford opportunity for the exercise of all the duties and obligations of citizenship."[24] Linking tolerance to citizenship began to be pronounced more and more. While loyalty, patriotism, and emphasis on school clubs were expressed, the promise and possibilities of democratic schooling surfaced.

6. Play and Democratic Living grew as a means to respond to the shortened work hours, creating unstructured and potentially delinquent activities among young boys. One of the aims of citizenship education rested on productive play through an appreciation of the natural environment and development of hobbies. The point of play was that it be a structured means of affecting outcomes for growth.

7. Changing Times and Ethical Principles attempted to lay out universal morals on which to base character. The authors' saw the "homely values" of honesty, thrift, loyalty, and tolerance as beginning points for facilitating discussion. These principles were not to be understood in a fixed and narrow way. Rather, class discussion was to provide a basis for that which proved too ambiguous.

8. Coordinating the Out-of-School Life required a smooth transition between social service agencies that looked to meet the needs of "problem" youth. The authors made it clear that schools were not a panacea for the problems plaguing youth and that a closer articulation between home and school was required for effective training in character. Outside organizations and community agencies, including churches, all needed to take part in raising the young. Thus character education required that all social forces, with schools providing one link in the chain, be held accountable in the production of future citizens.

The overarching theme expressed in *Successful Living* examined how schools, as laboratories of democracy, can facilitate the process of living a democratic way of life. To that end, the character education guide offered model programs in the classroom for emulation. Several examples of how model classrooms offered programs for character enrichment were highlighted in various chapters.

As for classroom practices, of particular interest were those offering quiet meditation, or "moments of silence," before the start of the school day.[25] This was meant to provide time for students to reflect on the day as well as to temper energetic bodies. Also, writing and composition were emphasized in the belief that "compositions created by pupils are the instruments through which we see their innermost souls."[26] Not only were there to be teacher-provided topics on which to write, but issues stemming from the lives of students were also encouraged. Above all, relevance between the subject matter of the composition and the experiences of students was needed. Lastly, the idea of homerooms generated much support in fostering citizenship and character. The bonds between teacher and students, and between students and students, were believed to flourish in a homeroom environment conducive to lasting relationships.

The guide's approach to tolerance was expressed through individual stories of students who came from various racial, ethnic, class, and religious backgrounds. The "success" stories focused on how important it was for students, especially immigrant and second-generation, to (1) recognize their cultural or religious background as one that has value and not as subordinate or inferior; (2) not denigrate their parents for speaking a different language and practicing foreign customs; (3) exhibit character at home by practicing the habits of citizenship, thereby serving as Americanizing agents to one's parents; and (4) understand that there are two sides to every story. Tolerance, or human understanding, was one way of countering various forms of maladjustments. To a large degree, however, the onus was on the immigrant or minority child to develop such habits of mind. When such habits were not fully actualized by the student, the Child Study Department, through their scientific assessments, found ways to address such matters.

Progressive approaches to character education, represented by *Successful Living*, reiterated old themes and introduced new ones. Although specific activities such as flag salutes and participation in civic clubs were not highlighted as much as they were in previous decades, broad notions of character education reflected indirect sentiments of loyalty and patriotism. The 1930s approach to citizenship education was characterized by an emphasis on the democratic way of life. Schools served to meet such needs through tolerance, open discussion, equalization of opportunities, and recognizing that students came to school with their own personal experiences. Whereas *Successful Living* served to foster character growth in and out of school, *Living Today—Learning for Tomorrow* provided the subject matter content for character development in the social studies.

LIVING TODAY—LEARNING FOR TOMORROW

Living Today—Learning for Tomorrow, published in 1938, was the Seattle Public Schools' curriculum guide for a course in social studies from kindergarten through senior high school. A course planning schedule, organized into semester-length sequences for the elementary and secondary level, provided a general description of the particular subject to be taught, including approximate time allotments for certain thematical issues, a discussion of materials for instruction—basic bibliographic listings, and the desired outcomes to be achieved for each grade and semester level.

By such a method of instruction, according to the guide, (1) The Student Learns about the World in Which He Lives; (2) The Student Experiences Civic Teamwork; and (3) The Student Gains Perspective and Lasting Interest in the World and Its People.[27] The emphasis lay in familiarizing students with their local geography and seeing how their place in the local community shaped things on a global level.

The major concepts that framed the social studies guide included mutual dependence, control over the environment, open discussion, obligations of citizenship, and preparation for democracy. Following are the major themes and issues teachers were to discuss in their classrooms.

Interdependence focused on the mutual dependency of individuals in that "Civilization is the product of the contribution of many races and peoples."[28] While not entirely focused on issues of interculturalism in the United States, this contention begins to address how society is composed of various cultures and ethnic groups that have contributed to the progress of its nations.

Changing Environment discussed the role of human nature's slow accommodation to changes in the environment and noted that "resistance to change and unreceptivity to new ideas often result in revolution by violent measures."[29] Perhaps reflecting on the political uncertainties of the time, especially overseas, this point served as a reminder that humanity needed to broaden its understanding in multiple contexts.

Man's Power to Control Nature was in some ways in response to the uncontrollable events surrounding the Depression. The know-how to build large-scale dams and projects manipulating the environment for human benefit became a battle cry of progress unlike social control, which remained modernity's "unsolved problem."[30] The centrality of human nature to manipulate its environment, particularly for "the betterment of society," is seen here as a commendable and worthwhile endeavor.

Obligations of Democracy called for the individual to participate in the civic duties of democracy, as voting was seen as a privilege with its own set of obligations and sacrifices.[31] The cost of freedom, in the eyes of the curriculum guide authors, was vigilance toward the common good.

Free Discussion, a variant on the freedom of speech, emphasized a critical component of democracy, especially in addressing the imperfect status of the government. Tolerance and striving for intelligent understanding through an exchange of diverse ideas was the bedrock of free discussion.

The Individual and Society addressed "man's" need to harmonize two opposing forces, one motivated by competition and the need to maintain one's individuality, the other by an obligation and responsibility toward society and recognition the need for cooperation.[32] The challenge of democracy lay in integrating both successfully: *e pluribus unum*.

The curriculum committee sought to have students comprehend and relate a connected historical narrative, recognize character traits of outstanding world characters (Moses, Socrates, Christ, Paul, Pericles), have knowledge of and respect for ancient texts, appreciate the long struggle for democracy, and have a sympathetic attitude to the long human struggle to improve and overcome obstacles in order to benefit society.[33]

The geography curriculum for these grades concentrated on an introductory study of the state of Washington as well as a strong recommendation to study East Asia. The main outcomes for learning geography lay in gaining a sympathetic understanding of other people from a study of their problems and an appreciation of how human beings, by working together, can, to a certain degree, control nature and improve conditions.[34] The idea that humans have the power to determine the fate of the natural and physical world was emphasized once again.

Successful Living and Living Today — Learning for Tomorrow represent a moderate, citizenship-based approach to character education and Americanization. Their progressivist outlook and method of instruction was, to a large degree, influenced by the national movements within the NEA and the PEA, especially in relation to character and social studies instruction.

As with many other curriculum guides, it is difficult to know or investigate the extent to which educators actually used them. At the very least, it may be safe to assume that teachers implemented a modified version of the ideas proposed, each teacher using what was most appropriate. Further, knowing how much the students actually learned and understood aspects of character education from their teachers is problematic as well. However, the students' letters themselves provide some evidence of how the lessons in democratic citizenship education were received, especially in relation to how their compositions, including their reflections on school assemblies, were recorded in their homerooms. The following section highlights, in greater detail, how homerooms, assemblies, and composition were critical factors in opening up the opportunities for students to write about their feelings.

THE CHARACTER OF SCHOOLING IN THE 1930S: HOMEROOMS, ASSEMBLIES, AND COMPOSITION AS VEHICLES FOR EXPRESSING INTERCULTURALISM

In Seattle and in various locations across the United States, schools adopted and adapted the concepts of homerooms and assemblies to achieve a sense of community and develop character education among the student body. The homeroom plan allowed teachers to monitor their students' academic and social growth throughout the school year. Homerooms also afforded opportunities for close relationships between teachers and students to develop. Naturally, close bonds between students also formed. The objectives of assembly programs were to instill and promote character education for students. The method for such instruction varied from school to school, but the objectives typically remained the same. In particular situations, as in the case of Washington School, students wrote about the content of their schools' assembly in their homerooms. Seattle schools in the mid-1930s emphasized the use of composition to further develop moral character and training in the habits of mind.

THE HOMEROOM PLAN

The 1935 character education guide for the Seattle schools, *Successful Living*, describes how the organization of the homeroom was an advantageous situation for teachers and students. Teachers were able to monitor their students' academic and social development throughout the school year. Having the same group of students, over an extended length of time, allowed teachers to examine their students' progress holistically. If a student's academic work slipped, the teacher was encouraged to look at environmental and familial situations by way of seeking improvement. The building of close relationships, going beyond the students' lives within the confines of the school, became a means of fostering character growth:

> Organization of the school into home rooms is often believed to be a decided advantage since it offers excellent opportunity for both direct and indirect methods of character instruction. Attention is centered upon the pupil, his activities, and his interests. . . . He contributes to the programs and the group discussions, which may be in the nature of direct character instruction but which are often closely connected with some school occurrence or project. . . . The child remains with the same home-room teacher during his enrollment in the school, and close pupil-teacher relationships are formed. The teacher learns the abilities, the interests, and the environment of each pupil and can give help in administering guidance to the members of his roll. . . . The members of the home room, working together for several semesters, create a group spirit. They develop a feeling of

responsibility to their group and to the school rather than to anyone who may commit a misdemeanor.[35]

To some extent homerooms and teachers were expected to serve as agents of social control. An underlying objective lay in diminishing acts of delinquency and heightening communitarianism. The introduction to *Successful Living* outlined a discussion on the potential risks of delinquent behavior. While schools cannot monitor a child's activities twenty-four hours a day, the argument went, "it can show him the rewards of evil doing, give him a sense of values, uphold high ideals, and teach him the scientific truths regarding the effects of such things as alcohol and narcotics."[36] The work of schools, within a homeroom atmosphere and beyond, would focus on education for character by providing the guiding principles for leading a moral and ethical life in and out of school.

In describing a segregated school in North Carolina's Caswell County, Vanessa Siddle Walker maintains that several features of the Caswell County Training School (CCTS) fostered an ethic of care and close relationships. Among those was the homeroom plan. "[It] was an important mechanism for facilitating relationships between teachers and students."[37] The teachers of CCTS felt that the homeroom plan provided for the sharing of lives, where in turn the teacher grew to accept and eventually have love for her students. Former students recalled their homeroom teachers as having a great amount of concern and care, creating a family-like atmosphere.

Walker's research provides a historical case study of how the concepts of homerooms and assemblies were implemented in classrooms and in the schools where a homogenous, ethnic minority, student body predominated. Former teachers, principal, and students supplied oral histories of their views of lessons received in their homerooms and school assemblies. Walker gives a historical glimpse into how the structure of schooling and school curriculum affected the lives of students. Similarly, my study incorporates evidence from students' writings—written in their homerooms—of how school assemblies affected them.

To clarify, while homerooms by themselves did not create caring communities, the combination of the teacher, the student body, the character of the school, and the neighboring community provided opportunities for caring relationships to develop. Although the particular case of CCTS, from 1933 to 1969, cannot be generalized to all public schools in the United States at the time, it nevertheless provides an important and critical insight into how the concept of homerooms played out. From *Successful Living* in Seattle to a segregated school in the South, homerooms potentially offered the space—at times intentionally—for close relationships to foster.

SCHOOL ASSEMBLIES

Along with the homeroom plan came school assemblies to further augment character and citizenship education. The purpose of assemblies varied in different geographic locations and across various cultural groups. However, a major thrust of school assemblies was framed around the development of character and group cohesiveness among the student body.

School assemblies in the 1930s in the Seattle Public Schools were seen as helping to unify the student body. They also held educative value. Discussions of various aspects of school life, descriptions of extracurricular activities, reports on citizenship clubs, and award ceremonies at the end of the school year were featured in the assemblies:

> Assembly projects serve to unify our purpose and carry out our building plans. An assembly program at the beginning of the semester acquaints the pupils with building aims and rules. Talks given by pupils tell of the purposes of the Girls' Club and Boys' Club, and such topics as the lunchroom, etiquette, and building courtesy are discussed. A welcome is extended to new members, and one of them responds. Another program given by the 8A class at the end of each semester brings to a focus the opportunities for character training offered by the school. One class used as its theme, 'The Character Side of the Report Card.'[38]

A focus on appropriate behavior for proper citizenship is clear. What is not included in this account of assembly projects is a message of understanding across cultures. Ideas of tolerance and the inclusion of ethnic groups' contributions to society were highlighted in detail in *Successful Living*. Whereas the assemblies were a unifying force for the student body, the classroom was the site of exploring different cultures' contributions to society. Model classroom programs for overcoming prejudice on the part of students (and not necessarily the teachers) toward immigrant cultures and ethnic minority groups are discussed in a chapter of *Successful Living* on what the homerooms can contribute in the organization of the school life.[39]

In Siddle Walker's research, school assemblies were called "chapels," a weekly gathering of students offering further means for education.[40] The weekly chapels at CCTS served two functions. The first was an extension of the activity program providing a focal point for club planning and gave students the opportunity to demonstrate their interests and exercise their talents before other students. The second served an educative function for discussing proper modes of behavior, as well as teaching about why particular historical events had direct relevance and significance in their education.[41]

Underlying these functions was the stress on character and moral principles. Principal Dillard of the CCTS often recited messages on the importance of character. The following excerpt is a yearbook address that best typified the content of the school's chapel:

> I can only say to you and ask of you that you hold fast to those enduring qualities which have been tested by time and eternity. Character is one of them. Character means confidence in one's integrity by others. It means worthiness, it means loyalty to the highest ideals of morality in one's daily affairs, it means the application of the highest ethical standards to everything you do, say or even think. Character is one of those precious spiritual commodities that cannot be bought, sold or traded on the open or closed market. One who possesses it has one of earth's most precious and priceless possessions. Seek it, find it, protect it.[42]

This excerpt provides insight into what an emphasis on character education might have looked like in a school's assembly. Principal Dillard of the Caswell County Training School emphasized how character as a virtue was tied to students' behavior and conduct, of which loyalty was one aspect. Character had to be nurtured and cultivated through careful instruction in the schools. The value of character education could not be measured like a commodity, but had to be acted upon through appropriate ethical and moral principles.

For intercultural educators of the 1920s and 1930s, character education played a secondary role to the cause of increasing intergroup awareness. Rachel Davis Du Bois, the pioneering intercultural educator, saw assembly programs as a way of promoting interracial harmony.[43] Assemblies were meant to appeal to emotions as well as intellects by enhancing classroom learning in a different way. As a doctoral student at Teachers College, Davis Du Bois conducted a systematic study on the effectiveness of assembly programs versus "incidental classroom teaching in developing tolerant attitudes."[44] From 1929 to 1930, she surveyed nine schools and four thousand students in the Philadelphia area and found that the assembly program was a more effective method for changing attitudes than a strictly intellectual approach represented by written materials.[45] She concluded, however, that the best approach to changing attitudes combined both. Perhaps realizing that assembly programs, along with activities in the homerooms, contained critical educative value for instilling all forms of character, including that of tolerance, the Seattle Public Schools worked to incorporate emotional and intellectual appeals.

LITERATURE AND COMPOSITION IN THE CLASSROOM

Successful Living articulated why a study of literature and composition augmented the development of character. Such an approach served two purposes: (1) to increase students' understandings of others' experiences through literature, and (2) to use writing as a means to express complex world situations. These dual objectives enhanced the growth of democratic citizenship.

Literature stirred the imagination of students by providing possibilities to envisage a moral life. In the Seattle schools, the writings of Louisa May Alcott, Maude Warren, Ralph Waldo Emerson, and Abraham Lincoln exemplified such goals. Certain kinds of literature not only provided a gateway for deeper understanding but also provided moral guidance—another critical component in the development of character. Writing about literature, and the lessons to be gleaned in leading a moral life, was a natural extension for character and citizenship.

Students' writings applied the lessons learned from literature to aspects of their own lives. As such, an example of an actual topic for classroom composition was "Where Was Your Dad Born?"[46] The objective in this writing assignment lay in appreciating the cultural background of an immigrant student through the study of his or her father. Examining the contributions of the country from which the students' parent immigrated deepened understanding of how world cultures were interconnected. The aim was to make the strange familiar. "The whole unit was worked out on the assumption that we seldom hate those we really know. Interest, understanding, and sympathy should first be developed, and from that, friendship will follow."[47]

A foreign language teacher in the Seattle schools shared her experiences for how she approached teaching tolerance. Her story, "Tolerance for Foreigners" was lauded for its appeal and effectiveness:

> I am glad in my foreign language work to have an opportunity to develop in the children a spirit of tolerance. In foreign books, I emphasize the fact that people of another nationality, though apparently so different from us, are fundamentally made of the same human stuff as we. They have the same emotions and therefore are actuated in much the same way. If all our children cannot be broadened by travel and personal contact with foreigners—their customs, their matter of thinking, and their ideals—at least they can read books which express these ideals.[48]

Despite the patronizing tone a present-day reader might detect in this passage, the emphasis on tolerance is clear. To clarify, the language of tolerance in *Successful Living* did not fully capture the complex multicultural fabric evident today. It was, however minute, a step toward recognizing ethnic differences in the Seattle schools. Literature would facilitate this process.

Composition extended naturally from the study of literature. According to the curriculum guide, writing was a gateway to one's conscience, a demonstration of how a student made sense of the world in relation to larger contexts as gleaned from literature. It was also an individual piece of creativity, generated from a unique understanding of immediate experiences. The process of composing built character and the principles for ethical and moral understanding:

> Someone has said that literature is the telescope through which we view human nature. We might add that compositions created by the pupils are the instruments through which we see their innermost souls. Their composition is a piece of creative work built by the student from his own thoughts. If we can help him to strengthen right ideals and can direct him to new avenues of high thinking, we create a condition that makes for fine character building.[49]

The writings by Nisei students add a critical dimension to the study of character education. Although the students' mode of self-representation through composition is mediated and complicated by sociopolitical and racialized contexts, we are, in essence, peering through the gateway to their conscience. While what they write may not be articulate and detailed, their expressions carry heavy meaning. Especially for Nisei students, their sense of self, or lack thereof, becomes salient. The Nisei students' affirmation of their American identities in the writings indicates that their identities were held suspect by others around them. The need to accentuate their loyalty to the United States came at a time when the government questioned Nikkei loyalty as viable citizens. The prejudices against Nikkei in Seattle and nationwide escalated within a few months' time. How students and schools reacted to outside pressures is revealed to varying degrees by the students' compositions and by the school district's response to wartime pressures. Ideas of understanding, sympathy, friendship, and tolerance once again surfaced as wartime hostilities and anxieties created tensions between Nisei and non-Nisei students. This crisis became a test of the schools' citizenship, tolerance, character, and democratic education programs.

Chapter 5

TENUOUS CITIZENSHIP:

SCHOOLS, STUDENTS, AND COMMUNITY

RESPOND TO WAR

★ ★ ★ ★ ★

SEATTLE SCHOOLS' RESPONSE TO THE BOMBING
OF PEARL HARBOR

December 7, 1941, has taken its place beside the dates in the life of America which will endure forever in the minds of the people. Never before in our history had there been so sudden and complete a transition from the ways of peace to the ways of war.

On the morning of the 8th of December Seattle teachers and principals began quietly and thoughtfully to meet the challenge. The need for calmness and orderliness was discussed with children who the day before had listened to the broadcasts from Honolulu and who had participated in the first hurried blackout precautions. Tolerance toward Japanese classmates was stressed. One principal reminded her cosmopolitan student body: "You were American citizens last Friday; you are American citizens today. You were friends last Friday; you are friends today."[1]

Sunday morning, December 7, 1941, was the day that would forever "live in infamy." Japan's bombing of Pearl Harbor in Honolulu, Hawaii, marked the entry of the United States into the Second World War. The "surprise attack" on U.S. soil by an Axis power heightened many Americans' fears of "yellow peril." The possibility of another raid by the Japanese grew in intensity and was exacerbated by the media. From the day of the bombing and into the incarceration of Japanese Americans, national magazines such as *Time* and *Life* published pernicious caricatures of the enemy Japanese that seeped their way into the minds of Americans of Japanese ancestry. Mainstream America could not distinguish between the Japanese of Japan and Japanese Americans who had lived in the United States for more than a generation. The fallacious representation that "all Orientals look the same" played out in full scale through the media's reports and pictorials juxtaposing Chinese and Japanese faces with the title "How to Tell Your Friends from the Japs." The friends, of course, were the Chinese, who at the time were considered an ally to the United States.

The bombing of Pearl Harbor ruptured any semblance of normalcy. Never before did the possibility of an international war occur so close to the continental United States. School officials knew that they had to address what occurred on Sunday when students entered school the following morning. As the *Seattle School's* newsletter indicates, teachers and principals prepared to meet the challenge by leaning on their tradition of democratic citizenship education. The school officials, within their sphere of influence, concentrated their efforts on promoting tolerance and citizenship, especially toward their Nisei student body. While they could not effect change in international politics, they at least controlled how their schools would respond to the United States' entrance into World War II.

In Washington School, Principal Arthur G. Sears had instilled democratic principles in his young students early on. In describing this role, and Sears's response to the bombing of Pearl Harbor, Martha Mortensen, a teacher at Washington, wrote, "The Principal, A. G. Sears, long ago laid the ground work for rooting out any existing prejudices. At all times he has tried to break down cultural barriers, establish mutual appreciation, and develop a program which would lead to a deep devotion to the American way of life. He has stressed a better understanding of all races and religions."[2]

Arthur Sears emphasized the teaching of democratic citizenship and tolerance at Washington School during his tenure as principal. His approach to the understanding of ethnic traditions was highlighted in a *Seattle Educational Bulletin* article in November 1937. The story described how Washington School students wrote individual letters to their parents inviting them to the school's open house. Many students were encouraged to write in English and in the language of their immigrant parents—Spanish, Hebrew, Japanese, or Chinese. Principal Sears explained this practice:

> I use this device not only to get the message over to the parents, but also to dignify the parental background. Too often I have seen tragedies among the second generations. They feel frequently that they have reason to be ashamed of their parents when they can neither read nor write the English language. I believe we produce better Americans from the foreign-born if we dignify their background, and while they should love America more, they should not lose their love of the land of their ancestry.[3]

Principal Sears understood the importance of preserving one's ethnic heritage. He conceded that total assimilation, at the cost of forsaking one's ethnicity, created a rift not only between the parents and their children but also within the children themselves. Thus a careful balance between one's past and present identities marked a successful entrée into the American way of life. Sears taught and maintained his views on the American way of life until his retirement in 1942.

WASHINGTON SCHOOL, 1941–1942

Washington School, where the writings by Nisei took place, bordered the multiracial Central District of Seattle, near a Jewish Settlement House, and served students from different ethnic backgrounds. The student body consisted primarily of Jewish immigrants from eastern and southern

Europe, Asian Americans and immigrants, and African Americans. Washington School, from 1920 until 1942, was among those which the highest numbers of Japanese American students attended.

From 1912 to 1938, Washington was a grade school. In 1938 it became a seventh and eighth grade center and remained so through World War II. In 1945 it became a junior high school. Washington, according to published reports, embodied cosmopolitanism. A 1961 Seattle school's publication described the history and tradition of the school as follows:

> Washington School, as a separate unit, in and of itself, presents a close approximation to the great American ideal which the fathers of the American Constitution hoped to achieve. A visitor to Washington School would find around one thousand children between the ages of 12 to 15, or every race, every religion, and every economic status, working together and playing together, with no tensions between them due to their differences of race, religion, or economic background. Democracy, in the true sense of the word, is practiced from the principal right down through the office staff and faculty, the custodians, and cafeteria workers, and then is reflected back again through the students themselves. The school is truly a small United Nations, actually accomplishing democratic objectives in an extremely significant way. Teachers and students are fortunate and privileged to be able to participate in the democratic situation as it exists at Washington at the present time.[4]

Washington School's philosophy of promoting democratic ideals is admirable, yet to maintain that no tensions existed between students remains questionable. The passage appears to be excessively romantic and borders on an imagined, color-blind democracy. Nevertheless, a survey of other schools' histories in the Seattle area revealed that only Washington explicitly emphasized the promise and possibilities of a democratic ideal. Certainly the character of the school, its teachers and principal, and the student body contributed to its unique reputation. Nisei students, through their compositions, expressed the extent to which that was real.

STUDENTS' REFLECTIONS ON THE SCHOOL'S ASSEMBLY
AFTER THE BOMBING OF PEARL HARBOR

According to the writings by Washington school students, and various Seattle school district materials, Principal Sears emphasized and stressed a democratic school life emphasizing tolerance and respect for differences: the dual appreciation of a unified political identity while recognizing individual and ethnic particularities as also expressed in the writings of John Dewey. The immigrant and ethnic group mix of Washington posed its own challenges, to be sure, and it appears that the principal did what he could to avert potential confrontations, especially in light of the bombing of Pearl Harbor. Sears's message of tolerance and recognition of all who make up the American ethnic composition is evident in the students' reflections. The students' interpretation of the bombing and the school assembly are foregrounded by what they were taught in schools and most likely by the values instilled in them by their family and community:

KEISOO—ENGLISH 7A1—DEC. 8, 1941
OUR ASSEMBLY

Today Mr. Sears talked to us about tolerance. As we know tolerance means to be friendly to other in any way.

When war broke out in the Far East situation yesterday some citizen of this country were intolerance. The people who are intolerant do not think before they speak.

Every person should be tolerant to different nationality if they have enemies.

FUMIKO—ENGLISH 7A1—DECEMBER 8, 1941
MORNING ASSEMBLY

The morning assembly was good for it tells to be good friends or neighbors wither our skin are different. That skin does not count by shelf but our spirit for helping people and cleaned heart count more for America and honesty too counts more for defending and best of all is love one another. We are all brothers and sisters even our parents and teachers but they are sent to take care of us and to give us more education and to become a better boy and girl.

The peom was good also and that all make to become American.

I wish sometimes if there were no war or evil thing, that do now happen were stop we sould be friendly with country more and more until the end of the world than people would be like neighbor, no war, no unclean heart, but all clean and cheerful voice in this world.

KATSU—ENGLISH 7A1—DECEMBER 8, 1941
THIS MORNING ASSEMBLY

In this morning assembly Mr. Sears experimented about having the morning assembly in the second period and next week it would be the third period because we always miss the first period class.

He spoked to us about not hating each other first because we have mixed nationalities in this school. But instead cooperate with each other and think of other people as our neighbors.

He also told us a story about a German boy and a Italian boy being a good American Citizens and even if their country is in war they are very good friends.

Mr. Sears read us a poem copied from a bulletin that a boy from Miss Fritzgerald's[5] room. Then he mentioned about the paper drive. After he was through with his speech we sang America from the bottom of our hearts and we also saluted the flag.

BETTY—ENGLISH 7A1—DEC. 8, 1941
ASSEMBLY

This morning we had a assembly in the hall. Mr. Sears told us that if even we have a different color face, it's alright because we're American Citizen. We all should be American Citizen.

He read us a poem of prayer because in school or out side the school the people might not be friendly with the other people which as (Japanese people) cause the war is going to be. When I heard Mr. Sears read that poem I was proud to be a American Citizen. And I'll (I am) always be American Citizen.

This year is the second world war in many years if it goes on.

When we were saluting the flag I was proud to salute the flag. Some people were crying because they were proud of there country.

The language of tolerance and citizenship, as expressed by these students, is clear. They understood Principal Sears's message of maintaining a steady course through friendship and understanding in the face of international turmoil. Their school needed to operate as a bastion of democracy. While teachers and administrators could not effect change in the community's response to the war—threats of increased racial violence—they could at least influence how students should act toward one another. Lessons in character and citizenship education became even more pronounced.

The meaning of citizenship weighed heavily on the minds of Nisei. Betty's statement "When I heard Mr. Sears read that poem I was proud to be a American Citizen. And I'll (I am) always be American Citizen" reemphasizes the importance of citizenship and an American identity. At a tenuous moment in her life she needed to remind her teacher, Ella Evanson, and herself that she, too, was an American worthy of the rights of citizenship. While Betty's teacher and principal taught those values, the government's exclusionary, race-based policy could not be changed.

The idea of difference and race, and how it fits within the concept of citizenship, was also foremost in the minds of the Nisei. The students' interpretations of race, either conceived by them or by Sears, were notable for their use of "different color face or skin" or "mixed nationalities" in their writings. In that regard, citizenship meant an acceptance of individuals from various ethnic backgrounds and racial characteristics, most notably differentiated by skin color. Race as a social and cultural construct permeated scientific communities and popular culture to create an artificial hierarchy of social order.[6] And for Sears to express the idea of equality of races, in spite of skin color, could have come as a surprise, as well as a welcome message, for some students.

The idea of race in the 1940s, especially in the Seattle area, can be understood in better context in the minutes of a 1939 meeting of the Council of Jewish Women (CJW) and in their work in the Settlement House near Washington School. One of the meetings of the CJW brought an anthropologist from the University of Washington to speak on Franz Boas's concept of the word "race" and why the term should no longer be used:

> Dr. Rose Ostrow introduced the speaker of the evening, Dr. Melville Jacobs of the U of W who spoke on "An Anthropologist's Point of View on Race." He explained that Dr. Franz Boas, noted authority on anthropology, urges the elimination of the use of the word race from the english [sic] language. He argues that there is really only one race on the face of the earth,—the human race,—that the gradual shadings from region to region are scientifically unjustifiable as "races,"—he suggests the use of the term "varieties" or "regional types."[7]

It is not known if Sears was directly influenced by the theoretical concepts of race at the time. However, his approach to racial tolerance was congruent with the ideas of leading anthropologists, such as Franz Boas and Ruth Benedict, who also influenced intercultural educators within the Progressive Education Association. Time and again, Sears's principles of racial equality, of one race—the human race, and the need for tolerance and brotherly love were reflected in the writings of Nisei and non-Nisei students. The students' compositions address how the concept of race should be focused more on the commonalities in the human race rather than on one's facial features.

The following set of writings reveals what non-Nisei students[8] felt about Sears's Pearl Harbor assembly presentation. They, too, expressed the idea that being an American encompassed an array of nationalities and skin colors, albeit slightly different.

EDMOND—ENGLISH 7A1—DEC. 8, 1941
OUR ASSEMBLY

This morning Mr. Sears us a good talk. "When we were friend, we love each other, but suddenly we hates each other maybe we had a fight or something else. This is same to school or between two nations. In school we were playing together, but some thing is not good, or the thing they don't like. And started to hate. War were broke out in the same way."

MAURICE—ENGLISH 7A1—DEC. 8, 1941
AMERICAN'S

In our first assembly, Mr. Sears our principal spoke on the freindly attitude toward the pacific crisis. He said, "We are all American's and we here at Washington want no part of race hated. We are all under the same roof."

In the short time he spoke he *accomplish* very much.

He spoke of 23 years ago, of how he work in the naturalazion dept., and of two gents (men), one a Italian and a German who at the same time as Germans were fighting Italians were still good neighbors and good americans. We should now be that way here at Washington school.

SHIRLEY—ENGLISH 7A1—DEC. 8, 1941
ASSEMBLY

In assembly this morning Mr. Sears told us about being intolerant he said that now because of the war different races might fight with each other and say that they started the war. He said that no matter what race or color you are that you are all American citizens and that even if your parent came from country that are fighting aganest us that we had nothing to do with it.

Mr. Sears also read a peom that a boy in our school made up it was very patreotic and expressed the feeling that and imagrant might have coming to America.

Mr. Sears said that people said to him that they thought he would have trouble with the children of Washington School because of the many different races and Mr. Sears said that he trust us and knew that we would not be intolerant.

GERALD—ENGLISH 7A1—DECE. 8, 1941
OUR ASSEMBLY

This morning Mr. Sears our principal of Washington School gave a talk about tolerancet. He said that we should not fight each other because their is nothing to fight about, ecsepth that the United States and Japan are at war but that should make little different because we are all citizens of American and citizen should not fight but be friend and help to make America a strong nation.

A noticeable distinction between the writing samples are the non-Nisei's use of the words "race" and "hate" in their reflections. In paraphrasing Principal Sears's speech, some of the students reveal, "'We are all American's [*sic*] and we here at Washington want no part of race hated [*sic*]. We are all under the same roof,'" and "He said that no matter what race or color you are that you are all American citizens." Although the underlying messages between Nisei and non-Nisei are similar, there are differences in the use of language to convey certain ideas. The Nisei students' writings indicate a level of internalization of being a proud citizen, especially in light of Sears's message of tolerance. In contrast, the non-Nisei student's summary of the school's assembly concentrated on what Sears said and not necessarily on what the message meant to the non-Nisei students. This might be an indication that the bombing of Pearl Harbor was "foreign" and distant from their experiences. One might imagine that they did not have to consider or question their status as citizens, for it was not a point of contention in their lives as it was for their Nisei peers.

In the non-Nisei's interpretation of Sears's assembly message, it appears as though the principal provided an analysis of the war by describing it in terms of friendships. As friends are prone to engage in disagreements and fights, he explained the war as once-friendly countries embroiled in a violent disagreement. The point of emphasis seemed to rest on Sears's insistence on not conflating the violence between countries at war with the bonds of intercultural friendships that developed at Washington School. Much like the tone of the passage that introduced this chapter, Sears stressed the importance of maintaining friendships among schoolmates.

The assembly concentrated not only on the bombing but also on the importance of examining citizenship in an all-inclusive framework. Principal

Sears reminded his students why differences in race or racial features should not be a means for discounting the rights of citizenship in the United States, even though the realities of war contradicted that idea. Sears, within his sphere of influence at Washington School, continued to emphasize the rights of all people who live in a democracy.

But in the weeks to follow, the community and the nation's responses to war and racial hysteria could not be quelled by school officials. The tensions and disruptions of the war permeated the boundaries of the school. The protective layer the school officials wanted to provide to students was wearing thin. The incarceration orders and subsequent removal of Nikkei became a focus of the media along the West Coast and became justified in the minds of mainstream America with the ever-prevalent phrase, "It was wartime and they looked like the enemy"—an oft-repeated phrase still used today.

THE COMMUNITY AND THE NATION RESPONDS

Newspaper reports from the bombing of Pearl Harbor through May of 1942 show the increased level of hatred and prejudice against Nikkei in Seattle and throughout the country. However, decades before the war, government agents scrutinized activities of possible "suspect" Japanese, and in the months before Pearl Harbor, the War and Justice departments prepared for their apprehension.[9] The immediate arrest of Issei and a few Nisei, including Buddhist priests, Japanese-language teachers, and community leaders by FBI agents on the evening of December 7, 1941, indicates the extent to which government officials were already prepared to take action. That evening, federal agents arrested 736 "Japanese aliens" in the United States and Hawaii, as indicated by the U.S. attorney general, Francis Biddle.[10] Most of the individuals arrested were taken to the jail at the Immigration and Naturalization Service building just south of Nihonmachi.[11] Clearly the swiftness and efficiency with which the government reacted hours after Pearl Harbor indicate the degree of readiness and preparation long before the bombing took place.

Shortly thereafter, the lives of Seattle's Nikkei, as well as Nikkei across the United States, were severely restricted. Seattle Japanese were being barred from travel on airplanes, buses, and trains on orders of the War Department and the Federal Bureau of Investigation.[12] An official U.S. Treasury statement suspended all Japanese financial transactions prohibiting the transfer of money or other assets to all Japanese regardless of how long they may have lived in this country continuously prior to June 11, 1940.[13] These major prohibitions occurred in the last days of 1941.

The restrictions against Nikkei also affected the lives of Nisei schoolchildren. The main Japanese Language School in Nihonmachi was closed by government orders. A *Seattle Times* article indicated: "Tokugo-Gakko Japanese Language School at 1414 Weller St. was closed yesterday for the first time since it was founded nearly forty years ago when its principal, Yoriaka Nakagawa, was held for investigation by the Federal Bureau of Investigation."[14] Considered a possible threat as an ally of the Japanese government, Nakagawa and other Japanese Language School instructors were arrested and later interned in U.S. Justice Department camps in Fort Missoula, Montana. However, in the same newspaper article, the aims of the Japanese Language School were described as promoting more the ideals of Americanism than loyalty to the Japanese government. Among the stated goals of the Japanese Language School in Seattle were to: "Study Japanese culture and always be correct, respect the elders and develop the virtue of obedience. Act with absolute sincerity. Develop the spirit of independence and become a good American citizen."[15]

Shortly after the bombing of Pearl Harbor many Nisei affirmed their citizenship by pledging loyalty to the United States. By this public act they sought to assure the public that they were not the enemy Japanese. James Sakamoto, the Nisei representative for the Seattle's Japanese American Citizens' League, publicly expressed the Nisei's "unswerving loyalty" to the United States immediately after the bombing of Pearl Harbor.[16] In a public ceremony on December 23, 1941 a group of Nikkei, mainly Nisei, gathered to pledge their loyalty to the government. The *Seattle Times* ran a photograph of the ceremony with the caption: "So massed that they overflowed into an adjoining gymnasium 1,300 Seattle Japanese are shown as they pledged allegiance to the American flag last night, and vowed to fight for American victory over their ancestral empire."[17] The local Methodist Preachers' Association Committee asked the public to regard the treatment of Seattle's Japanese by using "clear thinking and a Christian attitude."[18] Through late December of 1941 a tolerant attitude toward Seattle's Nikkei was expressed.

By February 1942, however, reports by the *Seattle Times* concentrated more on the increasing support to evacuate all Nikkei following the signing of Executive Order 9066. The *Times* reported, almost on a daily basis, arrests and raids on "suspect" Japanese,[19] the growing fear of another attack by Japan on the West Coast,[20] and various civic organizations and groups overwhelmingly in support of the forced removal of Nikkei.[21]

Once again, schoolchildren faced the brunt of many attacks against Nikkei. Toward the end of February and in March of 1942, Seattle's Japanese had to prepare to leave their schools and communities. In preparation for their removal, the War Department required that all Nikkei be registered. At Bailey Gatzert Elementary, the Lady Stirling chapter of the Daughters of the American Revolution eagerly joined in the war effort by fingerprinting all Nisei schoolchildren and issuing identification tags to children, many of whom were under six years of age and attending kindergarten and preschool. Ada Mahon, the principal of Bailey Gatzert, responded to the disruption of activities in her school by stating that:

> [n]o racial prejudice exists among students.
>
> We like to refer to our student body as "little democracy".... We attribute our success to the work of our Good American Citizens' Club,[22] which is made up of "upperclassmen" of the fifth and sixth grades. The students organize many committees, such as committee for clean grounds, good deeds, safety, clean shoes, turn-off-the faucets and activities like that.

The children are so busy helping each other, they have no time for developing prejudices.[23]

As much as Mahon attempted to show the public that the school reflected democratic ideals, one of them emphasizing tolerance, the young children "showed a strain of uneasiness over the uncertainty" of being forcefully removed.[24] Even for the young, the contradiction in the lessons of democratic citizenship with the news of having to be evacuated was a point of extreme dissonance. No longer were they looked upon as "American-born Japanese," but as the pejorative "Jap." As May 1, 1942, drew near, Nisei identities as Americans became conflated with the term relegated to the enemy Japanese. Despite Nisei efforts to prove their loyalty,[25] their imprisonment was imminent.

Newspaper reports in late March and in April of 1942 concentrated almost exclusively on the evacuation efforts being taken throughout Washington, Oregon, and California. Seattle's Nisei now turned toward cooperation with the evacuation effort as a sign of loyalty.[26] Resistance to the evacuation always existed among Nisei, and some questioned the democratic basis of the evacuation orders. And although many felt an inner turmoil, a mingling of humiliation, anxiety, and resentment, the removal process proceeded almost without incident, a fact that may be attributed to the Japanese stoic attitude toward adversity, *shikata ga nai*, "it cannot be helped."[27] By May 1, 1942, the majority of Seattle's Nikkei were bused to Camp Harmony in Puyallup, Washington.

Among those taken were the students of Washington School who wrote on what the "evacuation" might mean for them. Clearly, their lives from the time of the bombing of Pearl Harbor and into their imprisonment were affected by the events going on nationally and locally. Their schools became sites where democracy and dissonance came into play. The lessons of democratic life eroded into a reality marked by racial prejudice.

In the following chapter I attempt to capture the interplay of school, community, and national events through the oral histories of three Nisei, all of whom attended Washington School on the eve of their incarceration. Their life histories reveal how their identities were molded by how they viewed themselves and how others perceived them once the bombing of Pearl Harbor took place.

Chapter 6

★ ★ ★ ★ ★

The prejudice was coming out a lot more, I think, as the days went along.
There's the propaganda on the radio and then even at school when your own
friends are wearing these "I am Chinese" buttons . . . A lot of the friends that
you had were kinda ignoring you or keeping their distance.

—Hisa Kato, narrator

As the narrators of the oral histories will reveal, despite their schools'
attempts to quell prejudice and discrimination fomented against the Nikkei
community, the calculated attempts by the government, and subsequently
by popular media, to manufacture hate took its toll. The Nisei were Americans, yet their physical features precluded them from being regarded as
"complete" Americans. Indeed, the image being mirrored to them was one
of inferiority and incompleteness. Their political identities as "non-alien
aliens" played a major role, to say the least, in the formation of their self-
hood. Mitsie Fujii, one of the narrators, reflected that even after the war was
over, "I remember going to the mirror and looking at myself, at my face and
I think, 'Wow, do I look different? Do I look mean? Do I look bad? Because
right away you're stigmatized you think, 'Oh my God, you look just like the
enemy,' and you get scared. You don't know, cuz you're only what, eleven or

twelve? You don't know what's gonna happen, you don't know what the effect of all this is gonna be."

While evidence of what appeared in popular media and governmental directives is copious, what the schools were doing to address wartime hysteria is not that easily found. To be clear, I make no attempt to fill the gap in research on schooling prior to the evacuation. I wish to add a drop to the understanding of such complex events. My objective is to provide a historical case study of how the Seattle Public Schools and the students responded to the needs of its schoolchildren, particularly the Nisei, at a definable moment in the history of Japanese Americans.

The narrators tell a story of their lives prior to World War II and beyond and how schooling, if at all, helped make sense of the dissonance so evident in their lives. Their analysis and reflection of their own lives are common yet unique. Their shared history reveals how they came to problematize the idea of democracy, a concept that is very much taken for granted today.

ORAL HISTORY INTERVIEWS

The oral history interviews gather the personal accounts of surviving Nisei who attended Washington Junior High School; two of whom were in Ella Evanson's classroom. I asked them to reflect on their schooling experiences on the eve of the incarceration.[1] While their memories of schooling were at times vague, at best, their accounts nevertheless provided important clues on the Seattle Public Schools' tradition of citizenship and Americanization.

In approaching oral histories as a way to add to the dimensions of life within a community, I sought to make the public documents understandable through the narrators' recollection of the past.[2] While the analysis of primary sources makes for a compelling study in and of itself, the incorporation of the participants' voices add a new dimension of understanding that cannot be achieved solely through document analysis. Furthermore, how surviving Nisei saw themselves within the context of schools and commu-

Ella Evanson, in stylish dress, poses near downtown Seattle in 1942. She was the homeroom teacher to the Nisei students who wrote farewell messages on the eve of their incarceration. Evanson taught seventh and eighth grade English and Socal Studies at Washington School, and later became the school's librarian. (Courtesy Special Collections Division, University of Washington Libraries, Negative No. UW18876. Photographer unknown.)

Teruyo (left) and Sada stand in front of Washington School, days before their relocation to Camp Harmony Detention Center at Puyallup, WA in Spring of 1942. (Courtesy Special Collections Division, University of Washington Libraries, Negative No. UW18883. Photo by Ella Evanson.)

(From left to right) Yuriko, Emiko, Kazuko, and Chiyoko stand for a group photograph. (Courtesy Special Collections Division, University of Washington Libraries, Negative No. UW18885. Photo by Ella Evanson.)

(From left to right) Tokunari, Haruo, and Masaharu pose for their homeroom teacher, Ella Evanson, during their final days at Washington School. (Courtesy Special Collections Division, University of Washington Libraries, Negative No. UW18880. Photo by Ella Evanson.)

(From left to right) Yuriko and Kazuko manage to produce a smile for their teacher but Chiyoko has a distant, preoccupied look on her face perhaps too consumed with what she and her family will encounter. (Courtesy Special Collections Division, University of Washington Libraries, Negative No. UW18886. Photo by Ella Evanson.)

(Top: From left to right) Mary and Kazuko; (bottom) Reiko, Mary, and Yeoko enjoy their last moments with classmates and with their teacher. (Courtesy Special Collections Division, University of Washington Libraries, Negative No. UW18882. Photo by Ella Evanson.)

Students of Washington School prepare for visiting day at Bailey Gatzert Elementary on April 24, 1942. Most of the Japanese American students of Washington attended Bailey Gatzert, comprised mainly of Japanese and Chinese American students. (Courtesy Special Collections Division, University of Washington Libraries, Negative No. UW18884. Photo by Ella Evanson.)

Martha, one of Evanson's favorite pupils and with whom Evanson kept in contact through the 1970's, poses for her teacher. (Courtesy Special Collections Division, University of Washington Libraries, Negative No. UW18881. Photo by Ella Evanson.)

James stands in front of his school for the last time. (Courtesy Special Collections Division, University of Washington Libraries, Negative No. UW18887. Photo by Ella Evanson.)

Tooru sits pensively while Evanson takes a picture. Tooru was considered by Evanson, and his fellow classmates, as "the little professor." He was a talented writer and had a penchant for sketching ideas for his numerous inventions. According to some his former classmates, he died still unable to reconcile the anger and hatred that developed during World War II. (Courtesy Special Collections Division, University of Washington Libraries, Negative No. UW18879. Photo by Ella Evanson.)

The Shinto Church in Seattle's *Nihon-machi*, Japantown, where Tooru's parents served as Priest and Priestess. Evanson attended a number of ceremonies at the Shinto Church by invitation of Tooru. (Courtesy Special Collections Division, University of Washington Libraries, Negative No.UW18878. Photo by Ella Evanson.)

Pupils of Ella Evanson's seventh-grade homeroom stand at attention for a final class photo opportunity. Most of Seattle's Japanese American community was forced to evacuate by the time this photograph was taken. (Courtesy Special Collections Division, University of Washington Libraries, Negative No. MSSUA 472. Photo by Ella Evanson.)

Another farewell shot of Evanson's class in 1942. (Courtesy Special Collections Division, University of Washington Libraries, Negative No. MSSUA 473. Photo by Ella Evanson.)

nity helps in understanding the negotiation process of public culture. The in-depth interview can reveal a psychological reality that is the basis for ideals the individual holds and for the things he or she does: "How the subject sees and interprets her experience, given her view of herself and of the world, can be gleaned in no better way than to ask in the context of life review."[3] The point is not to gather the "truth" but to gain an understanding of how the narrators viewed and constructed their realities in a time of grave uncertainty. Further, it also points to ways in which their identities were constructed by their material realities of the time.

THE NARRATORS

Hisa Kato, Mitsie Fujii, and Kaz Ishimitsu graciously agreed to share an account of growing up in Seattle before the war. In 1942 they were thirteen and fourteen years of age, on the threshold of young adulthood. Their daily thoughts were consumed with socializing with their friends and going to school. National events such as a possible threat of a world war did not even enter the reality of their existence. To a certain degree, words such as "racism" and "discrimination" were not a part of their vocabulary. As long as they could remember, their attendance at Bailey Gatzert, under the guidance of Ada Mahon, and Washington School, with William Sears as principal, were among neighborhood friends, mainly other Asians, who did not think twice about contemporary notions of "difference."

However, the bombing of Pearl Harbor changed their realities drastically and in a most fundamental way. To this day, many historians of Japanese America divide a century of immigration and settlement into "before the war" and "after the war." The narrators, and most Seattle Nisei, share a common history. They were all born in Seattle bordering the International District, attended Bailey Gatzert Elementary and Washington School, intermittently attended Japanese Language School, were taken to the Puyallup Detention Center, were then transported to Minidoka incarceration site in

Hunt, Idaho, and resettled after the war in Seattle. Their common histories were bound by a legacy of discriminatory immigration laws beginning in 1790. The wave of immigration restrictions and subsequent settlement and birth patterns also gave rise to the distinct generational terms of Issei ("ichi"—one and "sei"—generation), Nisei ("ni"—two), Sansei ("san"—three), Yonsei ("yon"—four); first generation, second generation, third generation, and fourth generation removed from Japan, respectively.

Yet within the "common" stories lie individual voices of struggle, survival, and triumph. It becomes apparent that the age differences within the Nisei population had an effect on how schooling and the incarceration were experienced. Indeed, research studies on schooling in the camps were geared more toward the elementary and high school level.[4] The lives of junior high school students are usually combined with the high school experience and thus are lumped into a general category of analysis. Assuming that the experiences of adolescents and teenagers are or should be similar misses the complexity in the developmental consciousness and identity that students at the junior high level undergo. This difference of experiences within the Nisei is also in the narrator's account of their schooling. The point of emphasis here is that not all Nisei were alike in their feelings and experiences of the past. This is an obvious but important reminder, particularly in studying the lives of ethnic minority youth.

In an effort to provide a more honest account of the narrators' life experiences, long excerpts of interviews are provided with contextual analysis, as necessary. The purpose of this method lies in giving primacy of voice to the narrator and not to the author's interpretation of them. The "truth" of their experiences is not the aim, but rather how they construct the past through their perceptual lens, and how that construction of memory serves to formulate one's identity. Our memories, those events that reside in our consciousness, are constructed through the interplay of historical forces that shape our identities. The fact that some things are not remembered is just as telling as what is told in the story.

HISAKO "HISA" KATO[5]

Dear Miss Evanson,
I have missed your smiling face and I will miss you more, after all of
us are gone. I enjoyed being in your class a year ago.
With love,
Hisako Matsubara[6]

There is a certain level of calmness and balance in Hisa Kato's narration.[7] The perceptual landscape that encapsulates her memory bank is a complex web, yet she is able to provide a metacognitive view of things. She analyzes her memories by maintaining a level of "objectivity" and "distance." Hisa regards the actions of the past in historical terms with phrases such as "Well that was how things were in those days." She realizes that the world is completely different from when she grew up. She gives credit to today's youngsters for being "more sophisticated" and "worldly," in comparison with her experiences in the 1930s and 1940s. To Hisa and her family's credit, they managed to live on a single parent's meager income—even more remarkable considering that Issei were not allowed to own real property (the building or the land on which it was built) due to alien land laws. It is a tribute to the community, as a whole, that there were extended family members to help out as needed.

Hisa's recollection of the past, especially with regard to schooling, was certainly positive. Although her memories of Washington School are "like a blank," she does not think her experiences were very different from those at Bailey Gatzert. Since Nisei students of Washington were evacuated in March, April, and May of 1942, they were not able to complete the school year. That was a big factor in the lack of specific memories of Washington, Ella Evanson, and William Sears. Hisa's story, then, is one of a "normal" childhood disrupted by war and of her family's coping with the severe interruption in their everyday lives.

Hisako ("Hisa") Kato was born in 1928 in Seattle near the International District. She currently resides in a custom-made house built by her late husband in Seattle's Beacon Hill neighborhood. She retired from the Seattle Public Schools in 1990 and spends much of her days with her three adult children and friends, traveling, and doing volunteer community work. Hisa and her older sister were raised by her mother, who recently passed away at the age of ninety-four. Her mother earned a living managing a tiny candy store in Japantown. Because her father died when Hisa was only two, her mother was the family's sole provider. Hisa's family lived in a hotel-like complex that served as an apartment, located approximately one block from the candy store.

In retrospect, Hisa wonders how her mother managed to take care of her and her sister throughout those years: "We had everything we needed. It's amazing how my mom, with just that little candy store, raised us. We didn't feel as if we were neglected, or we went without, because we had everything we needed." Up until her schooling, Hisa spoke mainly Japanese at home: "... because at home, my mother didn't speak English that well and all the people who helped raise me spoke mostly Japanese. She [Hisa's mother] always marveled at how, especially the Nisei's, not just me, how we learned and got along in school." Hisa adds, "Of course I had an older sister and I learned from her."

Schooling Experiences. Hisa's formal schooling consisted of attending Bailey Gatzert and then Washington School prior to the evacuation. She went to Japanese Language School for two years and admits, "My Japanese is terrible, and I could just read the real simple, kinda like the alphabet type of thing. I can't read the fancy characters." She considers her comprehension of Japanese to be minimal. As was reflected by many other Nisei, attending of Japanese Language School, in addition to regular public schooling, was looked upon with great disfavor. They wanted to play after school rather than go to Japanese Language School. The idea of going to school twice each day was unbearable. This popular sentiment was aptly portrayed in Monica Sone's *Nisei Daughter.*

"So Papa and I have decided that you and Ka-chan will attend Japanese school after grammar school every day," She beamed at us.

I choked on my rice.

Terrible, terrible, terrible! So that's what it meant to be a Japanese—to lose my afternoon play hours! I fiercely resented this sudden intrusion of my blood into my affairs.

"But, Mama!" I shrieked. "I go to Bailey Gatzert School already. I don't want to go to another!"

Henry kicked the table leg and grumbled, "Aw gee, Mama, Dunks and Jiro don't have to—why do I!"

"They'll be going, too. Their mothers told me so."[8]

Sone's portrait of life in Seattle's Nihonmachi, especially in reference to Japanese Language School, evoked sentiments shared by many Nisei.[9] The description of her distaste for additional schooling resonated with Hisa and the narrators. However, the Japanese Language School had a powerful residual effect of creating close social ties among fellow Nisei's.[10]

In terms of her public schooling, while Hisa's memories of Washington are limited, she does remember the positive influence of Bailey Gatzert's principal, Ada Mahon. "I just loved her because she was very strict. But if you did what you were supposed to do, she was very nice. And I was quite studious so I got along quite well with her," Hisa reminisced. But it was a kind of "love" that spoke more of reverence, respect, and fear. Mahon was known as a strict disciplinarian. Students often marched down the hallways of the school, three abreast, synchronized to the chime of the triangle. Bringing "discipline" " and "order to things" was how Hisa framed her memories of Ada Mahon and Bailey Gatzert.

As far as citizenship and Americanization activities, Bailey had the Good American Citizens' Club and Hisa remembers being president for one year. They had assemblies reflecting on modes of citizenship. Citizenship education came in the efforts to imbibe a melting pot ideal. To that end, Mahon was central in promoting ways for her primarily Asian students to get along.

Perhaps due to the relative homogeneity of the school, socialization with other schoolmates came easily. Bailey Gatzert, as a neighborhood community school, contained an overwhelming majority of Asian students.

This was not so out of the ordinary, because the Seattle schools operated as neighborhood schools. And due to the "racialized" zoning of neighborhoods, most of the minority groups in Seattle resided along what is today commonly known as, the Central District:[11]

> So we went to school with Chinese kids and Filipino kids. We never had many Blacks in those days. So there was, you know, we were all mixed. I don't know why but we stuck around mostly with Chinese and Filipino kids. And it was only when the war started that the kids were told to wear these ribbons, I mean these little buttons that said, "I am Chinese." And that's when we knew about discrimination. Up to that point we weren't, we didn't feel like [there was] discrimination at all, because we went to school with them. They were our friends, and all of a sudden, whether the kids wanted to or not, the parents made them wear this, "I am Chinese" [button]. Other people, when they look at you, they can't tell whether you're Chinese or Japanese. I think we could but, as a whole you could kinda tell whether you were Chinese or Japanese.

Indeed, an Associated Press report indicated that Seattle's Chinese consul had ordered identification badges for all Chinese residents and citizens to wear, to avoid possible confusion and potential violence aimed against the Japanese. Hisa's sharp memory of this particular incident at school reflected the degree to which the mainstream public was not able to discern Asians of Chinese, Korean, or Japanese ancestry. The feared violence was not long in coming. The first reported attack, against a Nikkei, occurred in New York. Teddy Hara, a Nisei, was assailed by three unidentified men as they thundered, "Why don't you go where you belong?" before attacking Hara and leaving him with a skull fracture and lacerations and contusions of the left eye, face, and head.[12]

After the war ensued, Hisa remarks that divisions and an underlying racial tension did occur among fellow Asian groups and with Caucasian school mates and community people: "[A]t that age, you really don't understand it [discrimination]. But in those days [prior to the evacuation], we just went to school with our friends and they were all our friends." As with Hisa's and Monica Sone's accounts, a number of young Nisei did not think twice about "who" they were in terms of racial identity. They had always lived with, and were accustomed to, negotiating between their parents' Japanese culture and their adopted "American culture." Their lives between cultures were a matter of fact and not a matter of dissonance. This is not to say, however, that certain forms of "identity crises" did not occur.

Hisa's home life was fraught with worry about how her mother would be able to take care of her daughters with the news of the evacuation: "At that age, you don't have a voice about anything. You do what you're told to do. And if the government tells you you gotta leave, you leave." The "voicelessness" of many Nikkei members was also brought on by a feeling that there really wasn't anything that could be done. To show loyalty to the government by and large required doing what they were told to do.[13]

> As far as affecting the lives of the people, I think, if you were around, say, in the early 20s or something, just getting started in your life and, or just married or something, THEN it would've really affected their feelings, their thoughts, and everything. But when you're seventh-grade age, you know, you didn't worry about that kind of stuff very much.

Here Hisa realizes the age differences within the Nisei generation and understands how her personal experiences would be much different from those of her older counterparts. Being of junior high school age and heavily dependent on their parents precluded this group of Nisei from publicly protesting the level of injustice aimed against them. Feeling injustice yet needing to exhibit loyalty, Hisa and her family followed governmental orders.

MITSIE FUJII[14]

Mitsie Fuji's[15] recollection and representation of the past are explained with humorous anecdotes of how she and her family tolerated the bitter events of the war. She harbors no resentment for what happened. Rather, her buoyant personality underscores the strength she possessed to overcome that episode. What stands out in her narrative are the inhumane physical conditions at the Puyallup Assembly Center and in Hunt, Idaho. She describes in mild disgust the dust that permeated the air everywhere. It was as if the pervasive dust clouds, hovering above, were a telling omen for how everyday life would be for the Ideta family in one of the darkest moments of the history of this country.

In storylike fashion, Mitsie's memories weave and shift, back and forth, from camp life to life in prewar and postwar Seattle. Her overall recollection of Bailey Gatzert is favorable, as are her experiences with Ada Mahon. Mitsie attended Washington Junior High briefly before her family's departure to Puyallup. She cannot remember much of what occurred in Washington but does not believe that the environment there was much different from Bailey Gatzert's.

Mitsie now spends her days volunteering at a nonprofit agency founded by her daughter-in-law, and working on her computer. Her busy days are marked by quiet times of reflection on the past and the wonderment of how everyone was able to overcome such difficult times.

Mitsie was born in 1929 in Seattle. Her father left Nagasaki at the age of sixteen for Seattle.[16] Her mother immigrated from Hiroshima when she was seventeen years of age. She believes that her parents were married through an arranged situation (her father was twenty years older than her mother). Mitsie has two sisters (one of whom is deceased) and two brothers (one of whom is deceased). Her father started out as a plumber, became a salesman of wholesale fishing tackle, and later went into importing goods. Prior to the evacuation the Idetas lived in Seattle's Beacon Hill neighborhood. After a brief time in Hunt, Idaho's evacuation camp, the family lived in Des Moines, Iowa, for a year and a half. Mitsie is unclear as to how the move to Iowa occurred but thinks that her father's persuasive selling skills and abilities in business enabled her family to leave the camps earlier than other families. He even saved enough money to send his two eldest daughters to college:

> Because we were in camp, and he felt that we were wasting our time there he sent my two older sisters to school, college. And that took some bucks, I'm sure. I mean looking back now, at this age that I'm at, I wonder how they did it, you know, financially. But somehow he managed to send them to school. So, and actually as a matter of fact my dad researched three places before we even left camp which was unusual. And he researched three cities and he decided on Des Moines, Iowa. I think the other two he looked at were Chicago and Milwaukee, Wisconsin. But he decided Des Moines was a good place and it was a good place. The people were very nice and they'd never seen Asians before. I think they felt my black hair was such a novelty, you know?[17]

After the war, the Idetas returned to Seattle, where her father resumed his business.

As an eleven- or twelve-year-old adolescent at the time of the evacuation, Mitsie felt that she was not keenly aware of the ramifications and the seriousness of the situation but:

> I knew it was something drastic because we had to sell all our things and I'll never forget my sister, May, who was eighteen at the time, and this one dealer I guess came to try to buy stuff cheap. Everybody was trying to benefit from the hardships of the Japanese, you know like buying property, cheap furniture, cheap anything cheap because we had no choice, we had to get rid of it. And so this one man came to our house and offered us, and I remember we had this huge console radio that was just beautiful, and he offered us just a ridiculous sum and my sister she got so angry she told

him to leave the house, and I thought, "Whoa." And then we rode out to Puyallup the next morning and I remember sleeping out on the floor because we had sold off all the beds and things, there was nothing left. And got up and got in the truck I guess and took our one suitcase that we were allowed each and then left. And went to Puyallup and I thought, 'Wow, what a horrible place!' They had straw mattresses and then we had these barracks and then the partitions only went up so high so you could hear everything that was happening throughout the whole barracks and all the different families.

Clearly, Mitsie's recollections during wartime were of the stark contrasts between the everyday world she was used to and the dreary camp life that followed. She did not have a way of naming and articulating the situation into which she and her family were thrust, but she sensed the somber tenor of the times. Letters from the Puyallup Assembly Center to Ella Evanson also remarked on how the mattresses were made of straw and many different families had to squeeze into tight and confined areas. A popular sentiment held by internees was that the food and the diet in the camps did not reflect their cultural norms:

One of my most vivid memories was when my mom was able to cook rice on that pot-bellied stove and one of the things we love to eat was raw egg and soy sauce on hot rice. I mean it's just a real simple dish, but we *loved* it. And the first time I remember eating that in our barrack, with rice cooked at home, I don't think I'll ever forget it, it tasted so good! And then I remember the laundry rooms we had to go and just hand scrub everything, the sheets and the towels—Oh God that was awful. I don't know why my sisters weren't around it seemed like I was always the one that had to help her [mother].... Yeah Puyallup was pretty bad and in the wintertime it got so muddy and terrible...and the food. Vienna sausages, I'd never eaten Vienna sausages, they gave it to us I swear morning, night, and noon. And to this day I can't stand looking at 'em [laughter]. It's the funny things you remember, you know?

Her humor about camp food highlights a simple but major cultural disjuncture between a typical Japanese meal she was used to at home and the food at camp, which was most often heavy in starch, dairy, and processed meats.

Schooling Experiences. As far as schooling in Seattle prior to her family's departure, Mitsie attended Bailey Gatzert and then Washington School. She recalls that because Washington had set up a new junior high school system, she attended Bailey Gatzert for one quarter and then was transferred to Washington in January of 1942. Her memories of schooling, particularly of Washington, are not very vivid, but one instance at Bailey Gatzert stands out in her mind:

> I remember Miss Mahon saying to the Chinese kids not to wear those buttons saying, "I am Chinese." She was really offended because she felt that, we were all, you know, American citizens and all that. And the Chinese put them on to escape the wrath, the discrimination, and the anger from the White people towards the Japanese. But she, that assembly just really stood in my mind.

When asked to clarify the nature of the assembly and her move to Washington Junior High School, she explained in further detail:

> It was an assembly at Bailey Gatzert and she [Mahon] called the whole school together in the auditorium and, for the specific purpose of telling everybody not to wear those buttons. Yeah, so she was great. And then I remember going to Washington Junior High but really just for such a short time so it must've been for a month or so cuz we were evacuated in February in 1942. I remember the name of my teacher there [at Washington] I don't know why I remembered her but I think it's because I showed up one day in class and she looked at my dress and said, "What a pretty dress," and I thought, you know, because parents sold everything ... and my mom was always sewing dresses but I never thought anything of it. And I looked

to see what I was wearing. It was so funny cuz I couldn't figure out why she was saying that.

Mitsie remembers her teacher's name at Washington as Miss Mortensen.[18]

Mitsie's description of Ada Mahon was not very different from many Nisei recollections. She described her as stern but very fair. Her no-nonsense approach as an educator stands out in her mind:

> She was quite a person. She was VERY rigid, very rigid. I mean for as fair-minded as she might have been, she was also very rigid. But I think she was as fair as she could be in her position, I think she tried to be very fair. But she did run a very strict school. And I think the only reason it succeeded was because we were all children of immigrants, used to obeying, homogenous—pretty much, because I think the school was ninety-percent Japanese to tell you the truth; or Chinese...—but very few Blacks, very few Whites, so almost one-hundred percent Asian. Well, you know you get children at that age at that time, they're not boisterous and they're not, in fact I think I can remember out of that whole school, one or two or even three kids that were considered troublemakers. Also I think because of the Asian influence of real hard studying, hard working, smart kids, good students, and I think almost everyone did well in school. But she was strict, rigid, and that's why she was able to carry it off. I still remember everyday, dismissal time, we marched out of that school. And the song was playing on the speaker. I always, I liked her, but it wasn't a 'like' like you could just feel free to go up and hug her. Because she was like an officer in the Army, you just give them respect. I think the students were all in awe of her.

It appears that even at an early age, Mitsie was able to distinguish between an affectionate "like" and a respectful "like." She mentions how the cultural influence of her family and community promoted academic success in school. She also provides additional insight into how Mahon's role as a stern principal worked insofar as the student body comprised mainly Japanese.

Mitsie attended Japanese Language School, but for a brief time. Her experiences differ from the "typical" Nisei in this regard. She attributes that to her father's distinctive ways. Mitsie describes her father as being rather "unorthodox" and not caring too much about what others felt about him. "I kinda respected him for that because it is not easy to be like that . . . considering you're new to the country and you don't speak the language." And when it came to attending Japanese Language Schools, his attitude did not waver much:

> Well you know, my dad really didn't believe in them and so we started late. And I know all my friends went from the time they were kindergartners. And then he sent us to this one little school, rather than the one major school that everybody went to. So we went to this one small school and, it was really small, and I still remember the name of the teacher, his name was Ishi, and we called him Ishi-Sensei and we, I was just so old compared to the others in the class cuz you know we didn't start until late—I must've been in fifth or sixth grade and everybody else was in kindergarten. But you know, you at least learned the basics.

Mitsie reveals that the reason she and her sisters attended the small language school rather than the larger and more established Japanese Language School was that her father knew the instructor and wanted his children to go there. Aside from the embarrassment of a ten- or eleven-year old sitting among five-year-olds in the tiny classroom, she still was able to pick up the basics of the Japanese alphabet system.

The cultural encapsulation of living near the International District with fellow Asian youth did not allow for Mitsie to gain a sophisticated understanding of discrimination and racism. The homogenous environment with which she was familiar did not prompt the level of self-questioning that she remembers during and after the war:

> Well you know when you grow up, without knowing, when you're always with people of your own kind you don't really know anything about dis-

crimination because you don't experience it. And after the war I remember going to the mirror and looking at myself, at my face and I think, "Wow, do I look different? Do I look mean? Do I look bad?" Because right away you're kinda stigmatized you think, "Oh my God, you look just like the enemy." And you get scared. You don't know, cuz you're only what, eleven or twelve? You don't know what's gonna happen, you don't know what the effect of all this is gonna be.

Mitsie's realization that she was being looked upon as the "enemy" frightened her. She began to internalize part of the hatred and started to question who she was. The ambiguity stemming from the unknown ramifications of being allied with the enemy was a point of alarm and shame. She concludes:

And I still remember after we came back, I think it was in '44, '45, after VE-Day, and we were just, two of my girlfriends, I still palled around with mostly Japanese because that's all I knew. And these were all friends before the war and they had all come back. You see everyone had started coming back one by one, and as each person came back we didn't know if they were friends so we looked them up, and my girlfriend that was two years older than me, a childhood friend, was just living almost next door so I knew right away when she came back. And so we just picked up our friendship and started doing everything together again, even though she was a couple of years older but we still went to the same schools. And I still remember, the three of us were walking down 4th Avenue going past the public library and all of a sudden this woman turned to us and said, "Jap!" You know, just like that [emphasizing the offensiveness of the word] and we were just mortified. And I was just stunned but this other gal, she turned around and she said, "Fascist!" Oh, I thought that was so funny! So that was good for a laugh, we laughed about it. I thought, "Wow, fast thinking."

The racial epithet hurled by the woman on the street was indicative of the residual and continuous effects of racism. But in a remarkable and resistant fashion, Mitsie's friend responded with a stinging retort. This was, in effect, their own way of actively resisting and maintaining ethnic pride. Rather than internalize the pejorative nature of the word "Jap," the girls saw that the problem of racism resided in the woman and not themselves as inferior individuals.

KAZUO "KAZ" ISHIMITSU[19]

April 3, 1942
Dear Miss Evanson,
I cannot express the way I enjoyed being one of your formal pupils. I am sorry because I have to leave Washington School and miss you and Mr. Sears and all the teachers. I like to write to my favorite teacher but the time is getting short and I must close this letter.
Respectfully yours,
Kazuo Ishimitsu

Kazuo ("Kaz") Ishimitsu is very introspective and forgiving in his reflection on the past. He possesses a very spiritual outlook on his experiences while providing historical, political, and social explanations for why things happened the way they did. What stand out in his narration are the big questions of "why" and what possible reasons caused people to behave hatefully. He likens the diversity inherent in our society to the colorful flowers the "Creator" has bestowed in the floral beds of the earth. Kaz feels that it is the existence of all the beautiful colors that contributes to the well-being of all of us. The perspective he has now began as an adolescent in Seattle trying to make sense of the prewar hysteria. The only thing that made sense for him was developing a strong Christian faith of forgiveness and love. He also realizes now that the actions of the past stemmed from a racialized tradition of the United States reaching back to the Gentlemen's Agreement.

Kaz Ishimitsu was born in Seattle in 1929. He is the only surviving member of a family that included two brothers and one sister. His father,

Kichisaburo Ishimitsu, died when he was 105 years old. His mother, Yoshi Ashimahara, died when she was sixty-one, leaving her husband without a life partner for many years. Kaz's parents emigrated from the Yamaguchi area in Japan prior to settling in Seattle's International District. Although Kaz's age would indicate that he should be in retirement, his inexhaustible energy rivals any person many years his junior. He works full-time as a contractor, spends much time with his grandchild, and volunteers as a chaplain in a Nisei veterans' group. He currently resides with his wife in Bellevue, Washington.

One of Kaz's early memories of childhood comes from learning to sing Japanese songs his mother taught him. They had a gramophone on which to play the songs, but that was taken away by the FBI, as "evidence" of possible subversive, "fifth column" activities. "That was one of the first things the FBI took, this gramophone of all things, it's not a short-wave; it can't be used, in my opinion. No way could I imagine that could be used for sabotage, or you know, communication with the enemy. But that's the way it was. Somebody gained a nice little gramophone I used to learn my Japanese songs on." In one fell swoop a valued family treasure, which provided one of his earliest educative experiences, was stolen. To this day, he can remember some of the songs his mother taught him to sing.

Schooling Experiences. Part of Kaz's schooling experience included Japanese Language School. He remembers the burning of Japanese schoolbooks at the Japanese Language School he attended prior to evacuation. He attended for two or three years until the war interrupted his daily life. Like many other Nisei, however, he admits that he would rather have played baseball or football after school than attending Japanese Language School. He mainly learned the alphabet, the Kanji, and learned to read and write the rudimentary aspects of Japanese language. He, like Hisa and Mitsie, was taken to Minidoka, in Hunt, Idaho, after his family was bused to Puyallup for detainment. While in Hunt, he learned to draw blood as a lab technician at around fifteen years of age!

Kaz attended Bailey Gatzert and Washington School before the war. He has a vivid recollection of Ada Mahon and appreciated her sternness and strength as a leader:

> Oh, I liked her. She was a disciplinarian, absolutely. I know that she had probably a German background[20] I felt because … I'm very thankful to her because she made us march. Would you believe it? And when I was drafted in the Army now, I was a good marcher. I could march, I didn't have any trouble at all. It was wonderful, I learned march songs, I enjoyed it.

This almost amusing but utilitarian way of appreciating the daily marches at Bailey Gatzert is characteristic of the narrator's way of finding the good and practical lessons in any event.

He remembers another daily aspect of school life consisting of "prayer": "It was silent prayer, it wasn't perhaps strictly Christian or anything but we had a chance for silent prayer. The silence was there. The control was there.[21] We always gave the Pledge of Allegiance also. And we frequently sang the anthem, the Star-Spangled Banner; which was a difficult song to sing." Although not expressly stated by Kaz, these daily school rituals most likely served as an Americanizing tool for Mahon's students.

Today, Kaz's own view of "Americanism" is not the inculcation of a Westernized perspective, but rather a conglomeration of all philosophies. "It's taking the good out of all the different cultures.… Biblically speaking I apply it by 'you gotta like yourself.' You gotta know yourself and like yourself … self esteem is very important."

Overall, Kaz's memories of schooling are positive. In describing Ada Mahon's attributes as a principal, "She was strict. I think she showed enough love and care but her goal was to discipline, 'You've got to study,' that was the essential part of it, 'We're here to study, period.'" She also pushed students to engage in extracurricular activities, such as being a patrol boy or girl, and Kaz remembers being one and reflecting on how that experience, among others, helped to build his self-esteem. He remembers that while his schooling helped to formulate a strong sense of self, his esteem "was tore down *tremendously* during that war, that incarceration experience. That's the thing that really, I think it hurt many people. They became very 'Quiet Americans'[22] without being there to, none of that great big expression, you know."

In matters of self-esteem and how that was eroding away after the bombing of Pearl Harbor, Kaz remarks, "Well, if you read the Hearst papers or any of those, or listen to the radio programs, you know that they created hate....And because of that, they tell you you're 'slant-eyes' and all that, it was so predominant, 'yellow-belly,' that kind, it does affect the young mind." When talking to young people today, on how he learned to analyze his experiences of racism and discrimination during the war, he remarks how we are representative of the colorful flowers the "Creator" has bestowed on the world and how the intermixtures of those should create a system of love and care rather than hate. His view is that the more colorful the garden, the more opportunities exist for enjoyment.

The progression of the manufactured hate seeped into the community's perception of Japanese Americans, and Kaz remembers that it did not go away after the war:

> You could feel that you're the target of hate. They spearheaded that way and they, when President Roosevelt signed that 9066, I mean General DeWitt in charge, you know, he had a tremendous amount of this hatred. How it developed I don't know. But I know that members of the 442, following the war, asked him, "Well now what do you think of our achievements?" But he said that nobody didn't change his mind, "A good Jap is a dead Jap." He kept that attitude till the day he died. He had it embedded in him. It was an effort to make the United States ALL white."

His recollection of such military events are further informed by his experiences in the Army as a Nisei—although not in the 442d Regimental Combat Unit[23]—and his subsequent involvement in the veterans' group he serves as a chaplain. He keeps referring to diversity in humankind as flowers needing to express their beauty through their colors.

Kaz explains that fistfights, especially among boys, broke out in schools, although only occasionally:

> I had a friend, you know, he came along and says I'm a "Jap," you know. But they take on that, if you're a good American, that's what you do is hate the Japanese[24] it's the kind of philosophy that was built up.... You had a feeling of inadequacy. You're so much an outcast. That's the feeling ... As a citizen, what can we do to help? I don't like to kill. But yes, we had the occasional fistfights from anger. And get into fights, you know how kids get angry.

He recalls, however, that overall integration in schools existed. But moments of anger and violence erupted, especially as the Caucasian and Chinese American children were heavily influenced by their parents' perception of the war and who was considered the "enemy." Kaz explains that what would begin as name-calling escalated into fights. And being a typical boy, he himself did not let up or concede; although he admits that he could run pretty fast. In general, however, he wants to find ways to understand why the hatred was there.

One of the ways Kaz came to "accept" the everyday hatred of the time was adopting the Christian philosophy of love. As a young adult, he remembers attending church regularly and using his growing faith as a vehicle for understanding and compassion. It was the only way to make sense of the incongruence of the times. The level of irrational hate being produced became incomprehensible to a young mind, so a means of coping was to seek another level of understanding through brotherly love—a message Principal Sears of Washington School constantly urged his students to adopt.

Additionally, as an adolescent, Kaz was experiencing the typical process of identity development and group acceptance in and out of school, "You see as a young person, as you yourself could recall, you wanna be accepted. You

wanna be liked. You want to get yourself up in the world and be something."
He commented that one of the things that also helped him to get through
the tough times in school was the smiles of the teachers, "They always had
these nice smiles. Those I think took a lot of fear away." The simple, nonver-
bal act of care, as Kaz describes, was etched in his mind as a youngster
caught in an ambiguous space.

When asked to reflect on the importance of what it is that we should
remember in the Nisei experiences before and after the War, he explains,
"The things that I'd like to have people know [is] that we did kinda feel
badly as a whole because we were pledging allegiance, we used to, we
thought we were Americans. . . ." He refers to how it is the Creator's intent
for all of us to get along and learn from each other's culture and extract the
best from one another.

Kaz's vision of diversity and equality was learned by experiencing
racism. "It was TOUGH at times." Kaz illustrates this point by telling the
story of how his father, a carpenter, would get picketed by the union members for not being a member. Yet during that time, the senior Ishimitsu was
not able to join. Racist policies forbade Kaz's father to gain employment
security through a union. The sad irony in this situation erupted in violence
sometime later when two union members were trying to convince the
senior Ishimitsu to join, and Kaz's brother—who, later as an adult, was able
to change the union bylaws—spoke out, "Who in the hell are you to tell us
what to do?" Kaz goes on to say, "That night, they broke up the whole house.
We couldn't prove that they did it. You see that cost us a lot. They suffered
through, those are the sufferings that you have to deal with hate." So speaking up against injustice as a racial minority resulted in their house being
vandalized. The discrimination Kaz's family experienced was not totally
demoralizing. Through it all, his family and fellow Nikkei were able to
weather the various storms.

He attributes the endurance of the Nikkei community in Seattle to the
Issei values of strong family and communal ties that they brought over from

Japan as immigrants. The cultural milieu of valuing children, family, community, and education contributed to his social network of having other Nisei friends, although he does say that he had Jewish friends and others as well. Certainly, it is also the endurance and strength to overcome and live through the incarceration that helped the Nikkei to maintain strong ethnic roots.

NARRATORS' RESPONSE TO THE LETTERS

How the students at Washington School may have negotiated and reconciled their reactions to the news of the evacuation is further gleaned from an analysis by the oral history narrators. They were asked to freely respond to a sample of the students' writings as well as Ella Evanson's collection the author shared with the narrators. Their responses, then, are to the writings that resonated most with them.

HISA KATO

Hisa's first response was to the point in Tooru's essay that the evacuation would be for the "benefit of the United States." She agreed with what he had to say and added:

> I think that's how a lot of us kind of felt because we were, we figure we're Americans and we're Japanese, but we're Americans too. And of course, like, all the while we were going to school we saluted the flag of the United States. So well, we figure if the government thinks this is the best thing to do, that's what we *had* to do whether we like it or not. This is expressed really well in the first letter.[25]

The idea of "safety for their own good" and the threat of potential violence against the Nikkei community were real concerns. Sadako wrote, "I well start out my letter by writing about the worst thing. I do not want to go away but the goverment [*sic*] says we all have to go so we have to mind him." There were no real choices available for them. The idea, reflected in many essays, that "we have been asked to leave Seattle" is one rooted in the illusion of choice. They were forced to evacuate. Hisa understands that point made by Sadako:

> I think that's how we felt. We didn't have any power to change it. How do you even go about making changes at that age? Students expressed themselves real well for the age group. They wonder why? And you never got the answers. You don't want to go but you go because the government tells you you have to go. I think too, that maybe it's safer for us to be away from, because the propaganda was there's ships, because we were so close to the Pacific Ocean and everything. That there's submarines coming in closer and the ships are bringing troops in closer. Because the location [of where] Seattle was, not like you were way out in the middle of the country. And they kept saying that it might be safer for you [Nikkei] when you're away from the coast. So in a way, we thought, well maybe it is safer for us to go. And there was violence toward the Japanese, so we kept thinking, well maybe before things get worse it might be better if we do go kind of away where there's very few Japanese.

There was growing concern of the increased violence toward Japanese in the United States after the bombing of Pearl Harbor. Hisa noticed, too, that her schoolmates started to react differently toward her and her Nisei friends:

> The prejudice was coming out a lot more, I think, as the days went along. There's the propaganda on the radio and then even at school when your own friends are wearing these "I am Chinese" buttons. And I'm sure that the kids themselves didn't feel it that much but they were told by their parents not to associate with the Japanese students or something. A lot of the friends that you had were kinda ignoring you or keeping their distance.

Then I think too, I don't really know, but like the Chinese people especially, I think, were worried that they might be mistaken for Japanese. Because most Caucasians would not be able to tell a Chinese or a Japanese apart. And so maybe the parents were kind of concerned they didn't want their kids to be associating with the Japanese because they might be mistaken for Japanese. Little by little you start feeling scared. It's what you hear, what you see that kind of adds up to it. . . . It all builds up to a point . . . where something would happen.

Confounded by all the messages bombarding Hisa, she and her family and Nisei friends were overcome with feelings of fear. It was not a type of fear that happened all at once. Rather, it slowly built to a boiling point, as she aptly states, to "where something would happen." Her Chinese classmates and members of the Chinese American community in Seattle began distinguishing themselves from the Japanese by wearing badges that bore the phrase "I am Chinese." That was meant to signify for non-Asians that violence should not be aimed against a Chinese ally. A number of friendships were severed because of the message of hate aimed against the Japanese.

MITSIE FUJII

Mitsie was at Bailey Gatzert on the eve of the incarceration. She feels that the message from Sears in the school's assembly on December 8, 1941, was very much like the one Ada J. Mahon gave at Bailey Gatzert. She was caught by the phrase "not the Japs" in one of the farewell messages as one Nisei student was making a clear distinction between Seattle's Nikkei and the Japanese in Japan. She was taken by the students' ability to make that remark at that age.

Mitsie cannot recall any writing assignments on the incarceration, and it never dawned on her to write to her teachers at that time. The way she sees it, the idea of the evacuation was one that was too difficult to grasp in coherent terms, especially as a young person: "If we didn't grasp it, I can't imagine that they [the students at Washington] would." When asked how she thinks non-Nisei students might have viewed things:

> The way I look at it, the only impressions they would have I would think would be the ones that their parents gave them. They would, not follow the lead of their parents, but I'm sure take the direction from them as to how to react to it or what to think of it. Like we all do, you know? I must have been out of it. Obviously I don't remember that much.... When you're younger too, we were all so naive, I think compared to kids today that age. I mean such a world of difference. So if we were a little more sophisticated maybe I'd remember more but a little more worldly, but we lived in such a narrow world, small world, so that's about it.

Mitsie's life in Seattle's Nihonmachi did not lend itself to a diverse, intercultural experience. The racialized zoning of neighborhoods confined Mitsie and her fellow Asian community members to a particular location in Seattle. Hence her interactions with other peers in school and in the community were with other Nisei. Mitsie does not frame her life experiences and ideas of race and difference as a conscious reality. The war brought those issues to the surface. Mitsie's lack of specific memories of schooling prior to the incarceration is also a telling reminder of how, to a certain degree, her immediate reality was her small world of everyday life.

KAZ ISHIMITISU

At first glance, Kaz did not recognize his farewell note to Evanson. In fact, he glanced over his farewell message to Evanson without even blinking an eye. He says that he did not like to write and does not really remember his time in Evanson's class. His lack of memory for that time frame becomes readily understandable when he adds:

> At that time, there was a tremendous amount of fear, as a child. When you're going to lose everything, and you're mom is hurt bad and she cried,

"What should we do about the children? What kind of clothes can we bring for them?" We could only bring what you could carry...the parents concern was the welfare of the children. And of course there was anger, too. There was anger because we didn't do anything! What have we done?

To be sure, for some Nisei, schooling was perhaps the last thing on their minds. It also adds another complex component to the collection of writings. With all that the Nisei students were feeling at home with regard to the evacuation, did schooling have relevance in their lives? That is certainly an open question. However, Kaz does provide another important insight to consider in how students viewed their teachers at the time:

> Many of the teachers then really cared about teaching, really teaching. Miss Galen was my music teacher, I remember her at Bailey Gatzert day. But in Washington Junior High School I know that Miss [indecipherable] gave me a "D" when I didn't write a book report...I loved to play more than anything as a kid.

Kaz also remembers the bright smiles the teachers had and how that helped some students to cope. Many of the students' writings also mention how the teachers' smiles would be missed and that they would fondly recall their time at Washington.

Tooru's essays were immediately recognized by Kaz:

> This is my buddy, Tooru. I don't know what happened to this fellow. Oh yeah, he was a very, very smart man, Tooru was...he was a brilliant fellow. He passed away, he's gone. He wanted to be a like a teacher, a minister. He was too brilliant. He was a real thinker, a philosopher. I think he suffered a lot...all the hate, trying to comprehend what causes all this hate. What can be done? With that type of thinking. It's hard.

Hisa and Mitsie also recall Tooru as being a genius. It seems as though because of his unusually high intellect, he was at times ostracized by his peers. At the same time, however, the narrators remember having respect for his intelligence and deep reflection. According to the narrators, Tooru recently passed away.

Kaz did not specifically remember Principal Sears but remarks that the teachers and principals were "kind people." Upon reading some of the farewell remarks, he added how deeply upsetting it was to have to go. It further upset him that there was the possibility of his being recruited into the Army to kill people, which ran in strong opposition to his Christian beliefs. So for him, there were multiple reasons for his distaste for the war. Not only was he angry that his civil rights had been denied, he was also struggling with the idea that he might have to kill people for the war effort. The dissonance he felt at the time contained multiple layers.

CONCLUSION

The narrators provide information that is not easily understood in isolation. Their lives are contextually bound by a shared history of discrimination beginning with immigration policies up to the incarceration experience and beyond. There are predictable as well as unpredictable responses in their construction of the past. One of the salient points came in their positive experiences of schooling in Seattle, especially that of Bailey Gatzert and Ada Mahon. They all describe her as tough, stern, caring, and likable. They respected and held her in awe. They did not question too much their status as Americans because they grew up with fellow Asians and also with the schools' efforts to convey a thick, pluralistic description of democracy. While their memories of Washington School are not very vivid, they do sense that the attitude among the teachers and the principal did not differ from that at their elementary school. They remembered their teachers' ways of caring as exhibited through their smiles and moments of recognition.

While commonalities exist among the narrators, in terms of their shared past as defined by their ethnicity, their individual stories of their families were an unexpected surprise. I cannot imagine how Hisa's mother managed to care for her and her sister at a time when women's wages, especially for minority women, were barely sustainable. Yet, as Hisa remarks, her mother did what she had to do. As a child she did not feel deprived of the "normal" things children had while growing up. The strength of her mother and the social network of other Issei women in Japantown helped raise Hisa and her sister.

For Mitsie, she remembers her father not fitting the cultural norm. She tells a story of how when she was a girl her father, a salesman, took the whole family on a car trip around Washington State. One day for dinner, her father stopped in at what they considered a fancy steakhouse and ordered steak for everyone. What took Mitsie and her sibling by surprise was the moment when her father had the server take the steak back to cook as it was still mostly raw. As a child, she was flabbergasted by such a daring show of assertiveness. She was quite embarrassed and dumbfounded at her father's drawing attention to the family in such a way, but now she looks back on her father's act as a way of legitimating their presence in this state as viable citizens.

Kaz's way of looking back on his life and how past events came to be constructed in the way that they did provides deep insight into schooling and the incarceration experience. Despite the school's attempt to instill values of pluralism and democracy among the student body, racist acts emanating from the government and the media tremendously influenced the young mind, as he puts it. He feels that adolescents in their developmental growth need positive feedback about who they are and how they fit in society. Lacking that aspect at the time worked to diminish the self-esteem of many Nisei. The lessons from the past are the stories Kaz uses today in talking to young students about needing to appreciate who they are.

CONCLUSION

★　★　★　★　★

Seldom can schools change world events. At best, schools can offer opportunities for students to make sense of the dissonant world around them. Washington School, with teachers such as Ella Evanson and Principal Arthur Sears, provided a context in which to have students discuss, in composition form, how they were making sense of Pearl Harbor and the news of the incarceration. They instilled the lessons of democratic citizenship education that had been a tradition in the Seattle schools for many decades. While school officials themselves were powerless to overturn Executive Order 9066, they reminded their students that everyone was an American. Homerooms, assembly programs, and composition opened up the space for students to learn about democracy and citizenship, and to express the lessons learned.

Through the students' written expressions, many powerful ideas emerge. Nisei students emphasized their loyalty to the United States regardless of the outcome of their lives. As citizens, they trusted in the government. Schools continued to remind their students that everyone was an American, regardless of which countries were at war with the United States. However, many Nisei still faced chaotic home lives. Some of their fathers were arrested by the FBI and interned in Fort Missoula, Montana. Many of their mothers were left to resolve the final details of their removal from Seattle. Most of their belongings had to be sold. Family memorabilia were either burned—for they might have been deemed "suspect" by the FBI—or sold to the lowest bidder.

For non-Nisei students, they themselves had to face the idea that their friends would soon be gone. They also trusted the government to take care of their schoolmates. "After all," as one student wrote, "we're all American citizens but the children with Japanese ancestors will have to be evacuated." The distinction between "American" and "American Japanese" became more apparent at this time. Despite the fact that Nisei were citizens, they were imprisoned for looking like the "enemy." *Shikata ga nai*, it cannot (could not) be helped. Students' letters from Camp Harmony in Puyallup revealed the increased level of dissonance between the life they knew versus their new life in a makeshift horsestall:

Puyallup Assembly Center
D-1-22
Puyallup, Wash.
Dear Miss Evanson,
   How are you and are you having a good time? I am but I'm getting quite lonesome because I am missing my studies. Although there isn't any school over here I use some of the studies I was taught by you and now am I glad. Since I came here the only thing you could do at home is to study and write letters so when I begin writing letters I take all the steps I learned.
   Now I will be closing for I will have to write to the 7B3's so Good bye and Good Luck
A pupil
Yeoko

B-2-48 Camp Harmony
Puyallup, Wash.
May 10, 1942
Dear Miss Evanson,
   How are you? I am fine, but I had my Typhoid shot and now I have a headache, and my arm aches.

I arrived in Puyallup, Friday. We passed Kent, Auburn, Sumner, and then to our camp. I guess your wondering why we came here so late. Well, we were delayed because we had to go to the Clinic.

We have to make our own chairs, and tables, and the mattress for the bed with hay in it. (Isn't it terrible.)

How is the class? Are there any Japanese in the class (7B3) like Yeoko Yamaguchi? If she is there would you ask her for her address?

We eat from 6 to 7 (morning) 11:30 to 2:30 (afternoon) 5 to 6: o'clock in the evening.

The shacks are cold and has holes in between the logs. Our place is in Camp B.

Your friend,

Mary

P.S. Please write to me, and the class also because it is lonely here. May I have your picture too?

These letters stand in bitter irony in relation to the Thanksgiving Day letters students wrote in November of 1941:

Nov. 17, 1941   Fumiko
English   7A-1

WHY I AM THANKFUL

I am thankful for my father and mother who take care of me and give me food and clothing. I am thankful that I have a house to live in and that I am healthy. I am thankful that I could go to school, have shelter, freedom of religion, to live in America, and kind leader that is not a dictator. For teachers, friends, sister and brothers who encourage me when I am sad and well make me happy.

I am grateful for flowers, birds, trees, rivers and valleys to make everyone enjoy them all for God also wants to make us happy.

We should not only thank God once a year but everyday should be a day for thanking Lord because there are so many many thing to be thankful of in America.

Nov. 17, 1941   Katsumi
English   7A-1

WHY I AM THANKFUL

I am thankful because I have a mother and father who care for me,
while in Europe there are some children who do not even have a
mother or father to care for them.

There are many good reasons why I should be thankful. I am
thankful for the home I live in and the country I live on. I am thankful
because I can go to school and work without fear of airplanes flying
over our heads dropping bombs.

I am thankful for the beautiful city I live in with clean drinking water,
good school buildings, beautiful parks, playgrounds, etc.

The strength and persistence of Nikkei to survive the years behind
barbed wire fences is also a testament to their faith in the power and
promise afforded in a democracy—especially during a time when the government proved to be undemocratic. The Civil Liberties Act, signed by
President Ronald Reagan in 1988, acknowledged the findings of the U.S.
Commission on Wartime Relocation and Internment of Civilians that the
imprisonment of Japanese Americans was motivated largely by racial prejudice, wartime hysteria, and failure of political leadership.[1] Nisei and Sansei,
second- and third-generation Japanese Americans, spearheaded the
Redress Movement to seek personal justice for every individual incarcerated during World War II. They reminded the general public that democracy
was not in force. American citizens were denied due process, and the forced
imprisonment of innocent civilians was a serious breach of democratic principles—rudimentary lessons all students learn in schools.

Democracy, loyalty, citizenship. These were the very lessons taught in
the Seattle schools from 1916 until the time of the Japanese American incarceration. The first superintendent, Frank Cooper, laid down a tradition of
steering a moderate course in response to Americanization pressures.
Cities across the United States represented a range in how Americanization

programs were implemented. Some places fought hard to implement English-only practices and required their immigrant students to conform to Anglo standards, while others offered a more social welfare approach in the assimilation process. In Seattle, Superintendent Frank Cooper early on resisted the efforts by Daughters of the American Revolution and the Minute Men to control school curricula and activities devoted to patriotism and loyalty. Cooper also stood firm in favor of not erecting a permanent school building for immigrant students with limited English proficiency. A relevant curriculum, and not rote learning, was his main pedagogical emphasis in schools. Seattle schools also served the needs of immigrant communities by offering night classes on Americanization and English language instruction. All of these curricular and extracurricular components laid the foundation for a progressive approach to Americanization and citizenship education through the 1930s.

The Great Depression of the 1930s and the international political upheavals redirected ways in which schools should educate for democratic citizenship. Educational organizations and their leaders in the National Educational Association and the Progressive Education Association emphasized the need for character education. Tolerance and a push toward intercultural understanding was a major thrust for character and citizenship. Seattle schools, through curricular and extracurricular content, also employed similar concepts to educate their students on the values of civic ideals.

Successful Living and Living Today—Learning for Tomorrow were the primary character and curriculum guides used in the Seattle Public Schools to promote ideas of tolerance and intercultural understanding in a democracy. Influenced by the PEA and the NEA and the intercultural education movement, the Seattle schools, and Washington School in particular, drew on the progressive intercultural framework in responding to the events of Pearl Harbor and the incarceration. *Successful Living and Living Today—Learning for Tomorrow* are evidence of an early form of multicultural education in the Seattle schools.

With the news of the bombing of Pearl Harbor and the signing of Executive Order 9066, schoolteachers and administrators acted as moral agents by conceiving of their own agency in the context of injustice. They knew that the political forces of the Second World War and the incarceration could not be stopped. Many teachers and administrators privately dealt with the message of democracy and dissonance on their own. However, they knew that the principles of democracy, on which the Unites States stands, needed reinforcing, especially for their Nisei students. Ada Mahon, principal of Bailey Gatzert Elementary, ordered her Chinese students to take off the "I am Chinese" badges distinguishing them from Japanese students at the assembly after the bombing of Pearl Harbor. While Mahon could not effect change in the community's actions toward wearing identification badges, she realized that in the context of her school, she had the power to control how democratic principles were to be understood.

Likewise, Principal Arthur Sears of Washington School in his school's assembly made it known to his students that everyone was an American. The need for brotherly love rather than hate was required. He warned his students that there would be the possibility of violence against Nikkei outside of school, but that he trusted his students to reach for understanding and tolerance—the basic lessons of citizenship the students learned in school. Early on, Sears understood the need for immigrant schoolchildren to appreciate the cultures and values of their parents. The most healthy form of democratic citizenship education was one in which students learned to combine aspects of their cultural and "American" values.

The early forms of multicultural education, through an emphasis on interculturalism and tolerance, proved a lasting and important lesson for Nisei today. The oral history narrators recollected their time at Bailey Gatzert Elementary and how the simple lessons taught in schools, with the support of extracurricular clubs such as the Good American Citizens' Club, helped to foster an identity where discrimination did not play a big role. While aspects of the "color-blind" philosophy was in force at the time in the 1930s and 1940s, especially with an emphasis that the only race that existed was the human race, many students did not think twice about notions of race and difference. As the oral history interviews indicate, it was not until the war and the news of the incarceration erupted that they were faced with feelings of inferiority.[2] Their early schooling played a big part in how they identified as Americans. Subsequently the war made them confront the lessons of democracy learned in school with the dissonance of being treated as an alien enemy.

How schoolteachers and administrators of Seattle Schools reacted to wartime events has direct implications for teaching in multicultural contexts today. How do we teach for democratic citizenship when forms of racism and discrimination still exist? What can schools do to foster ways for students to express their innermost souls? How do we teach for ambiguity? Seattle schools, and Washington School in particular, were faced with these very questions. School officials did not know what would happen with the war and with their students about to be imprisoned. They knew, however, that one of the ways for students to confront these uncertainties was by writing about that which affected their lives. The curriculum of the school had to connect with the realities the students were facing. Homerooms and school assembly programs provided opportunities for students to express these realities. However uneasy and tenuous the situation was, school personnel had to address how one was to live with such ambiguities. Much of what happened at Washington School can be credited to a principal and teachers who looked to a caring-centered, social justice approach to teaching.[3] The principal and teachers knew what would happen to their Nisei students following the signing of Executive Order 9066. Yet despite that looming inevitability school officials emphasized the democratic principle of equality by caring for those directly impacted by the incarceration order.

Schools cannot change the scope of international politics or the structural inequalities of our society. Even at Washington School their model "United Nations" could not sustain its fragile democracy. On September 25, 1968, the Seattle School District closed Washington Junior High because of racial tensions.[4] Schools at the time became sites of contestation following the larger move towards social and structural equality. Civil rights leaders questioned the extent to which schools truly reflected the aims of democracy with its practices of segregation and tracking along racial lines. The color-blind philosophy of the early twentieth century no longer held sway. Beneath that veneer lay an unsteady platform built on systematic racism—an issue school officials then (and now) were too willing to eschew.

That the aim of democracy exists alongside much that is undemocratic is an everyday reality that all students, at some point, must face. At best, schools can offer the space of hope, the promise of what democracy can offer in the face of injustice and ambiguity through an explicit discussion of ongoing undemocratic practices. Through such lessons we can envision the possibility of what could and should lie ahead, an increasingly democratic society with increasingly democratic relations.

A NOTE ON METHOD AND SOURCES

★ ★ ★ ★ ★

THE HISTORICAL QUESTIONS

This book examined how Washington School, the site of a Deweyan experiment in intercultural democracy, dealt with the challenge to its experiment by the news of the Japanese American incarceration. The following questions, based on a historical investigation of primary evidence, framed my study: What ideas of democracy, Americanization, and citizenship were expressed in the writings by Japanese American and non-Japanese American students from 1941 to 1942? In what ways did students and school officials cope with a federal policy calling for the imprisonment of Japanese Americans on the West Coast in light of citizenship education based on tolerance? How did Japanese American and non-Japanese American students make sense of the contradictions between the citizenship education they received in school, on the one hand, and the prospect of the incarceration on the other? These research questions served as the basis for conducting a historical analysis of primary evidence based on students' writings, archival documents, and oral history interviews of Nisei who attended Washington School.

REVIEW OF RELEVANT RESEARCH

While the study of ethnic minorities and immigrant groups and their relation to public school education during the Progressive Era and the Great Depression are plentiful,[1] there are still relatively few accounts of the West

Coast experience. As a result, relatively few sources provide accounts of the schooling experience of Asian immigrants who figured prominently in West Coast cities. Also, some studies look at the history of schooling on the West Coast but focus primarily on school organizational policy, paying little attention to student populations. The existing studies of Seattle schools fit this latter category.[2]

The two major exceptions to this general description are Judith Raftery's study of reforms in Los Angeles schools[3] and Eileen Tamura's work on Americanization and acculturation of the Nisei generation in Hawaii.[4] Both these studies give considerable attention to issues of Americanization and discuss the relationships between ethnic communities and schools, with Tamura focusing specifically on Nisei. However, both end their accounts before World War II and neither deal with the question of how the meaning of Americanization changed or was challenged by the West Coast's peculiar experiences during the war. Seattle provides a rich context for taking on this topic, especially as it contained one of the highest percentages of Japanese Americans in the United States at the time. Other than the landmark study by the sociologist S. Frank Miyamoto on the Japanese community of Seattle,[5] there is yet to be a published study on the schooling of Japanese Americans in Seattle. My study thus addresses research on schooling in Seattle from the perspectives of students and school officials on the eve of the Japanese American incarceration. This scenario presented a ripe case to study Americanization and citizenship education in the context of a governmental policy of exclusion.

Another body of relevant historical literature is on the incarceration—especially that which explores the responses of Issei and Nisei to the fact of being incarcerated. The body of literature stretches across disciplinary fields and literary genres. Major historical works are *Years of Infamy: The Untold Story of America's Concentration Camps*[6] and *Japanese Americans from Relocation to Redress*[7] which includes autobiographical accounts of Issei and Nisei during the incarceration. Roger Daniels, who has written extensively on the history of Asian Americans, has written specifically on the incarceration experience in *Prisoners without Trial*[8] and on the history of Japanese Americans. Gary Okihiro's *Whispered Silences*[9] tells the story of the camps from reminiscences of former internees. *Personal Justice Denied*,[10] the report of the Commission on Wartime Relocation and Internment of Civilians, with a foreword by Tetsuden Kashima, is based on the congressional hearings and includes the evacuees' account of their lives behind barbed wire. Oral histories gathered by Arthur Hansen,[11] John Tateishi,[12] and Densho: *The Japanese American Legacy Project*[13] provide rich repositories of research. Exemplary works focusing on Nisei are Robert O'Brien's *College Nisei*[14] and Bill Hosokawa's *Nisei: The Quiet Americans.*[15] Yuji Ichioka's study[16] of the Issei is arguably the definitive historical work on the immigrant Japanese. Local histories of Japanese Americans include Kazuo Ito's *Issei*,[17] James Watanabe's *History of the Japanese in Tacoma*,[18] Linda Tamura's *The Hood River Issei: An Oral History of Japanese Settlers in Oregon's Hood River Valley*,[19] and Thomas Heuterman's *The Burning Horse: The Japanese-American Experience in the Yakima Valley 1920–1942.*[20] A more general history of Asian Americans can be found in the numerous publications by historians Ronald Takaki and Sucheng Chan.

My study is different, however, in placing the events prior to the incarceration in the context of school lessons on Americanization. I trace the development of the Seattle Public Schools' official declaration of citizenship education from 1916 to the changes of attitude and approaches through the 1920s, 1930s, and early 1940s. This book explores the schools' and students' reactions to the impending incarceration within the backdrop of the tradition of Americanization and citizenship education training. While previous studies focus on the incarceration experience itself, I concentrate on the schools' and students' response prior to the event.

There are two major aspects of the history of education to which this research project will contribute: (1) the social history of education as reflected in the experience of the participants themselves—the students;

and (2) the history of Americanization and citizenship education in the West Coast context of Seattle Public Schools.

A project centering on what students felt and expressed during a time of war addresses a major gap in historical research. Too often, the voices of students are rendered silent and not given due recognition. What role schooling might have played with respect to one's identity is a major concern for Japanese American students, whose loyalty and citizenship status were held suspect. The question of what it means to be an American loomed heavily for those whose identities were at stake. Focusing the study on what students wrote places them at the center, and not at the margins, in the social history of education.

Second, the issue of how schools reacted to wartime events, on the basis of a tradition of teaching tolerance, puts to the test the idea of democracy and citizenship education. The theory and practice of democratic life had been an explicit subject of discussion in the schools, and thus the challenges the U.S. war policy made to those ideas may have been particularly salient in the school context. Not only did the students have to make sense of the dissonance, but school officials and teachers did as well.

DEWEY AND INTERCULTURALISM IN THE SEATTLE SCHOOLS

In framing how students responded to wartime events, I looked to the tradition of progressivism—best reflected in the philosophies of John Dewey—in the Seattle schools. While the opportunity Evanson provided her students to express the grave circumstances facing their lives is important, it is equally important to examine whether the culture of expression was open to all students.

In that vein, I have found that Washington School, which the students of my study had been attending at the time of their incarceration, was in the late 1930s and early 1940s the site of a Deweyan experiment in intercultural democracy. I look at what happened to this experiment when its ideals were tested by the news of the incarceration of the Japanese American students.

In this investigation the following three ideas have helped to frame my thinking: public schools as laboratories of democracy; democracy as a mode of associated living; and public culture as a product of historical negotiation.

Public schools can be sites of experimentation in democracy.[21] When coupled with Dewey's definition of democracy as a mode of associated living, which includes intercultural recognition, the experiment becomes that much more complex:

> A democracy is more than a form of government; it is primarily a mode of associated living, of conjoint communicated experience. The extension in space of the number of individuals who participate in an interest so that each has to refer to his own action to that of others, and to consider the action of others to give point and direction to his own, is equivalent to the breaking down of those barriers of class, race, and national territory which kept men from perceiving the full import of their activity.[22]

This idea provides a framework for understanding how Seattle Public Schools, in general, and Washington School, in particular, became a site for the negotiation of public culture across social differences of race and culture. According to Dewey's philosophy, schools needed to reflect and model a laboratory of democracy, working to guard against students leading miseducative experiences. An educative experience included a mode of communicated existence based on an understanding of difference.

The Seattle Public Schools in the 1930s looked to Dewey's philosophy to guide their school life. The districtwide resource guide for character education and democratic schooling, *Successful Living*, included the following commentary in its "School and Democratic Living" section:

> Any program designed to attack the real problems of living must help to prepare the individual for successful living in a democracy such as ours. He must learn how to work with others for the common good. The school, serving all the children of all the people, has a unique opportunity for overcoming snobbery, reducing racial and class prejudices, and teaching the

brotherhood of man. The individual must gain a consciousness of his civic responsibilities. Dewey reminds us of the fact that school is not only a preparation for life; it is life itself. It may be so organized as to afford opportunity for the exercise of all the duties and obligations of citizenship.[23]

As this statement indicates, school officials saw schooling as an opportunity to put democratic principles into practice. An important element in the school's concept of democracy came in reducing various forms of prejudices. The authors of the guide—a group of social studies and history teachers, as well as administrators—were clear to point out that school is more than mere preparation for life. Schools needed to model a democratic life in a way that Dewey envisioned. While the Seattle Public Schools attempted to outline a democratic way of life, Washington School was recognized for its reputation for modeling democracy.[24]

Other primary source evidence in the 1940s points to Washington School and its principal, Arthur Sears, as trying to model a Deweyan idea of democracy based on an appreciation of difference. The students represented varied ethnic and religious backgrounds, ranging from Japanese and Chinese American, to African American, Jewish, and members of other immigrant groups. Sears specifically addressed these differences and how students should regard each other as equal citizens in a democracy. The claim that the school actually achieved a condition in which "no tensions" existed between students due to differences of "race, religion, or economic background" is questionable, to be sure. But it is clear that this vision of intercultural democracy was the ideal or model Washington School set for itself. In this regard, the school strove to model a laboratory of democracy.

To expound on the idea of public schools as "laboratories of democracy," it can be argued that opening up opportunities to deliberate on issues of social and political import is paramount. Public schools offer a public forum for deliberation on public issues. At the most positive end of the spectrum, public schools can be models for effective democratic citizenship education through recognition and appreciation of individual and group differences. In the most negative view, public schools can perpetuate and re-create racial, gender, and class stratification.

Seattle Public Schools' administrators and teachers were aware of approaching democratic school life as a form of laboratory. A 1940 *Seattle Principal's Exchange* issue addressed newer instructional practices devised by the Department of Supervisors and Directors of Instruction. The idea of schools as laboratories of democracy was pronounced:

> If we do not believe thoroughly in democracy we should not talk it so much or lead parents and others to expect a degree of democracy in education which we have no intention of delivering.
>
> The school is thus a laboratory in which one lives, studies, discovers, tests, and enjoys the democratic way of life. It is a laboratory in which the pupil, through living, broadens his sympathies for all human beings, enlarges his faith in humanity, and increases his capacity to see merit in the uniqueness of other personalities. It should be a laboratory which serves as a home base for the exploration of all phases of society outside the school. It is a laboratory for living and testing the method of science, of intelligence in the solution of problems. It is a testing ground for criteria of truth and value. It is a creative environment in which unique personalities can flower.[25]

That the schools were to educate for a democracy through the laboratory method was clear. It was meant to test and broaden one's skills and perspectives while helping to develop the unique character of each individual in a democracy. It was, above all, a means to explore one's humanity.

In light of the laboratory view of education, it is also fair to equate that perspective with an experiment; and in a laboratory, experiments may succeed or fail. The results are not entirely predictable. This is where the notion of public culture comes into play. If one thinks of schools as laboratories of democracy, then they represent a kind of public culture where national and local events are brought to the fore for possible public deliberation. In that context, the deliberative process accounts for varying perspec-

tives that are predictable as well as unexpected, peaceful and violent, tolerant and intolerant. As careful as one may be in conducting an experiment in
a socially controlled environment, the possibilities for human "error" clearly
are vast.

Public culture, then, provides another lens for understanding how
Washington School represented a minidemocracy for negotiating issues of
moral and social import. Thomas Bender's idea of public culture helps to
frame the case of Washington School as a historical event:

> Very recent historical scholarship however, is beginning to reveal a public
> realm that is not a given but is, rather, a product of historical processes, one
> made and remade in time. The process of making and remaking supplies a
> focus for a new historical synthesis. How do different groups contribute to
> that making? How are groups defined in their relation to that culture? How
> do groups gain (or not gain) legitimacy? How do they participate (or not
> participate) in the creation and distribution of public meaning and institu-
> tional power? The key to such synthesis is an understanding of difference
> in America that is relational, that does not assume discontinuity in social
> and individual experience.[26]

Bender's critique of the failure of recent historical scholarship to
address the interrelatedness of historical participants to larger political and
social forces becomes useful in the analysis of Washington School. The
question of what happened in this particular experiment with democracy is
a historical question. It requires that the concept of public culture be his-
toricized, that it be treated not as a static event, but as a historically contingent encounter negotiated and renegotiated in different ways in different
times by different people. This book examines the process of negotiation
and renegotiation of public culture in Washington School at a time where
the very ideas of democracy and citizenship were being tested. If Washington School was a laboratory of democracy, the democratic experiment
underwent a severe test in the winter of 1941–1942. The news of the forced

imprisonment weighed heavily on the Japanese and Japanese American, Nikkei, community all along the West Coast. The subsequent fears of another attack by Japan and growing rumors of Nikkei espionage—encouraged by the government and the media—were overwhelming realities. In spite of what seemed to be a hopeless situation, the teachers and principal of Washington School used their spheres of influence to remind students of the importance of democracy and equality. My study examines the historical forces that influenced the process by which Washington School and its students, administrators, and teachers coped with the news of the incarceration.

DATA AND METHODOLOGY

Data on the Seattle Public Schools' policies on Americanization come from archival research of superintendents' memoranda, district newsletters, annual reports, and curriculum guides. Documents spanning nearly two and a half decades from 1916 through 1942—with materials focusing largely on the 1920s and 1940s—make up this book. The year 1916 marks the start of this historical analysis as specific Americanization and citizenship training policies and curricula are discussed and given primary import in the Seattle Public Schools' *Annual Reports*. Other cities and states also began Americanization programs at this time. The year 1942 concludes this analysis as the United States' entrance into the Second World War disrupted many school activities on the West Coast, especially with the forced removal of Japanese Americans. Also, within this twenty-six-year time span, the greatest influx of immigration, subsequent anti-immigration policies, and increase in birth rates, especially among Japanese residents and Japanese Americans, occur in Seattle and throughout the West Coast.

Examining the scope of Americanization policies in the Seattle Public Schools lays the historical context for what the schools were teaching up until the time of the incarceration. The students' response to wartime events and the reaction to Executive Order 9066 contain elements of what the schools were teaching all along. The school district's emphasis on American civic ideals provides a perspective for beginning the examination process. The school district's *Annual Reports*, the *Principals' Exchange*, and the superintendent's memoranda all speak to promoting an effective citizenship education based upon civic values and responsibility for democratic living.

Secondary case studies of Americanization programs nationwide complement the historical focus on the Seattle program. The general scope of Americanization ideology and citizenship education played out in various ways across various regions over time. While specific actions and policy measures ran the gamut, the overarching theme—that of instilling in students the "American" way of life—contained an Anglo-Saxon standard. From Honolulu, Hawaii, to Gary, Indiana, efforts to assimilate and acculturate were steadfast.

ANALYZING STUDENTS' WRITINGS

Analyzing written work by students requires a healthy dose of skepticism. Many educators would agree that whenever classroom work is assigned, varying degrees of resistance and noncompliance exists. Whether in historical or present-day contexts, students' active and passive resistances to requisite work are a matter of fact. The case for Ella Evanson's students is no different. The collection of students' writings indicates levels of depth and superficiality. Some are highly descriptive and emotional while others are not. A myriad of factors comes into play when relying on students' writings.

Without a doubt, the students' voices, especially those of Nisei students, need to be taken into account in this analysis. Possibly realizing that they were writing for an audience, the students might have felt reticent to disclose their true feelings—much akin to the public acts of compliance and general acceptance reported by the news media. Cultural characteristics might also have played a factor. Emotional restraint, or *Enryo*, was a value passed down to Nisei by their Issei, or immigrant, parents. To disclose one's feelings in public was seen as a sign of weakness and lack of respect. While not all Nisei adhered to this value, *Enryo* was a cultural trait largely understood by most Nikkei. The students' writings are also bound by the local and national attention to the war and the media's increasing efforts to project hate toward Italy, Germany, and especially Japan. The blurring of identities between Japanese and Japanese Americans became ever more apparent in the eyes of other mainstream Americans. This in turn prompted many Nisei to project hyperloyalty to the United States.

Observing how students responded in writing to traumatic versus non-traumatic events revealed that, by and large, Nisei reflections on the events after the bombing of Pearl Harbor and their farewell entries were different from their regular classroom writing performances. Students showed a more personal side of themselves in talking about traumatic events in contrast to the more generic responses associated with writing about Thanksgiving Day, for example. In the following essays written by Nisei on "Why I am Thankful," it becomes apparent that they repeated much of what the teacher and/or the principal told them. Nearly all of the students' writings sound the same and address the same issues (freedom of religion, thankful for family, not living under a dictatorship, having plenty of food to eat):

WHY I AM THANKFUL

I am thankful for my father and mother who take care of me and give me food and clothing. I am thankful that I have a house to live in and that I am healthy. I am thankful that I could go to school, have shelter, freedom of religion, to live in America, and kind leader that is not a dictator. For teachers, friends, sister and brothers who encourage me when I am sad and well make me happy.
I am grateful for flowers, birds, trees, rivers and valleys to make everyone enjoy them all for God also wants to make us happy.
We should not only thank God once a year but everyday should be a day for thanking Lord because there are so many many thing to be thankful of in America.

WHY I AM THANKFUL

The reasons I am thankful are (1) because we don't have two slices of bread daily because of dictatorships like in Europe (2) I have my parents and elders to care for me (3) I can go to any church I feel like (4) listen to any radio program during any time and read any newspaper, magazine, or comic books.

Instead of waking up at nights fearing enemy planes will drop bombs over our head we sleep soundly at night never caring what time we wake up.

Seattle is an industrious city with beautiful parks. We can enjoy the climate as it is not too hot nor too cold. Public schools where we study so we can be good business men or women instead of running to the air raid shelter when we hear the siren.

Seattle has their own baseball team which we go at nights to see and enjoy ourselves. Besides Seattle we have the huge United States of America, the land of freedom, that is the main thing I am thankful for.

THANKSGIVING

This Thanksgiving meant more to me than any others because I could have a home, when others in Europe don't and we do not have to hear those terrible noise and try to run away for fear of bombs. I thanked God for the wonderful things that he has provided for me that I could worship freely, and be healthy, and warm in my home.

I thanked God and said that the people in Europe many be having food, clothing, and a warm home, and terrible noises away from them and have peace in Europe for they too want be free from noises and not be ruled by dictators but their own ruler, and many rule for them and many have peace in the world for ever and ever until the end of the world.

The bitter irony in these essays lay in the students' appreciation of living in a democracy, where they possess a number of freedoms. Yet within a few weeks' time, their lives would be altered by the very government for which they gave thanks.

APPENDIX:

CHRONOLOGY OF EVENTS AFFECTING

JAPANESE AMERICANS NATIONALLY

FROM DECEMBER 7, 1941, TO JUNE 7, 1942[1]

★ ★ ★ ★ ★

1941

December 7   Japan attacks Pearl Harbor.

Authorized by a blanket presidential warrant, United States Attorney General Francis Biddle directs the Federal Bureau of Investigation to arrest a predetermined number of "enemy aliens" classified as "dangerous." This list includes Japanese, German, and Italian nationals. By the end of the day 737 Japanese are in federal custody.

December 8   The United States declares war on Japan.

December 11   1,370 Japanese classified as "dangerous enemy aliens" are detained by the FBI.

December 22   The Agriculture Committee of the Los Angeles Chamber of Commerce recommends that all Japanese nationals in the United States be placed "under absolute Federal control."

December 29	All enemy aliens in California, Oregon, Washington, Montana, Idaho, Utah, and Nevada are ordered to surrender all "contraband." "Contraband" includes: radio with short wave bands, cameras, binoculars, and a variety of weapons.

1942

January 5	All Japanese American selective service registrants placed in Class IV-C along with enemy aliens. Many Japanese Americans already in military service were discharged or put on "kitchen police" or other menial tasks.
January 6	Los Angeles Congressman Leland Ford sends a telegram to Secretary of State Cordell Hull urging the removal of all Japanese from the West Coast. Ford wrote,"I do not believe that we could be any too strict in our consideration of the Japanese in the face of the treacherous way in which they do things."
January 28	California State Personnel Board votes to bar all "descendents of natives with whom the United States [is] at war" from all civil service positions. This rule is enforced only against persons of Japanese ancestry.
January 29	Attorney General Biddle issues the first of a series of orders establishing prohibited zones which must be cleared of all enemy aliens. German, Japanese, and Italian aliens are instructed to evacuate areas on the San Francisco waterfront.
January 30	California Attorney General Earl Warren calls the Japanese situation in California the "Achilles heel of the entire

civilian defense effort." He further states that "unless something is done it may bring about a repetition of Pearl Harbor."

February 4   The U.S. Army defines twelve "restricted areas." Enemy aliens in these designed areas must observe a curfew (9 P.M. to 6 A.M.), and are allowed to travel only to and from their place of employment. In addition, they are forbidden to travel any further than five miles from their place of residence.

February 6   A Portland post of the American Legion circulates a resolution urging the removal of all "enemy aliens, especially from critical Coast areas." The cover letter attached to the resolution indicates that the post is urging the removal of all Japanese regardless of citizenship.

February 13   In a letter to the President, the West Coast congressional delegation urges the removal of "all persons of Japanese lineage . . . aliens and citizens alike, from the strategic areas of California, Oregon and Washington."

February 14   Native Sons of the Golden West urges the evacuation of all Japanese, regardless of citizenship status.

February 16   California Joint Immigration Committee urges that all Japanese be removed from the Pacific Coast and any other areas designated vital by the U.S. government. FBI arrests and detention of Japanese aliens reported to be 2,192.

February 19   President Franklin Delano Roosevelt signs Executive Order 9066. This order gives the secretary of war the authorization to establish military areas "from which any or all persons may be excluded as deemed necessary or desirable."

February 20   Secretary of War Henry L. Stimson appoints Lieutenant General John L. DeWitt as the military commander responsible for executing Executive Order 9066.

February 21   Hearings by the House Select Committee Investigating National Defense Migration (Tolan Committee) begin on the West Coast to investigate problems of enemy aliens and others living along the Pacific shore.

February 26   All Japanese on Terminal Island, San Pedro, California, are given forty-eight hours to evacuate homes and business by naval order. They are allowed to resettle where they can.

February 28   House Committee on Un-American Activities makes public its Yellow Book. The 300-page document contains almost every possible charge against the Japanese in America.

March 2   General DeWitt issues Public Proclamation No. 1 designating military areas in the states of Washington, Oregon, California, and portions of Arizona. It further states that certain persons or classes of persons might be excluded from these areas should the situation require it. The restrictions apply to Japanese, German, and Italian aliens, or any person of "Japanese Ancestry" living in Military Areas No. 1 and 2.

March 16   General DeWitt issues Public Proclamation No. 2 making Idaho, Montana, Nevada, and Utah Military areas No. 3 through 6, respectively.

March 18   President Roosevelt issues Executive Order 9102 creating the War Relocation Authority (WRA). Milton S. Eisenhower is named the first director and charged with the task of implementing a program of orderly evacuation of designated persons from the restricted military areas.

March 21   Congress enacts a law providing penalties for persons who violate orders to enter or leave the designated military areas.

March 23   Civilian Exclusion Order No. 1 is issued by General DeWitt. It directs that all persons of Japanese ancestry, both alien and non-alien (American citizens) evacuate Bainbridge Island near Seattle, Washington, on or before March 30, 1942.

March 24   Public Proclamation No. 3 extends travel restrictions, curfew, and contraband regulations to Japanese Americans, regardless of citizenship.

March 27   Public Proclamation No. 4 issued by General DeWitt. It prohibits the voluntary evacuation from Military Area No. 1 by Japanese aliens.

April 7   WRA director Eisenhower meets with the governors or representatives of ten states at Salt Lake City. States represented [are] Nevada, Idaho, Oregon, Utah, Montana,

Colorado, New Mexico, Wyoming, Washington, and Arizona. The meeting is to ascertain the views of these states on accepting Japanese evacuees. Only Governor Ralph Carr of Colorado offers to cooperate.

May 7   National Japanese American Student Relocation Council is organized through the efforts of the American Friends Service Committee. The council is designed to assist evacuee college students to continue their education outside the proscribed military areas.

May 8   Evacuation of all Japanese living within the Arizona Military Area is reported completed.

May 16   The Atlantic Coast is declared a military area by the Eastern Defense Command.

May 21   Initial group of incarcerated Japanese Americans leave the Portland Assembly Center to do agricultural work in Eastern Oregon.

June 7   General DeWitt announces that the removal of 100,000 persons of Japanese ancestry from Military Area No. 1 is completed.

NOTES

★ ★ ★ ★ ★

INTRODUCTION

1. Exemplary works are included in the "A Note on Method and Sources" section.
2. Carlos Bulosan, *America Is in the Heart* (Seattle: University of Washington Press, 1943/1996), 147.
3. As a point of clarification and accuracy, I shall be using the terms "incarceration" and "imprisonment" rather than "evacuation" and "internment." According to David Takami, in *Divided Destiny: A History of Japanese Americans in Seattle* (Seattle: University of Washington Press and Wing Luke Museum, 1998), "Evacuation" was a government euphemism for the forced removal of Japanese Americans on the West Coast. It conveyed the idea that the removal of citizens was for their own safety. "Internment" is a technical term applied to prison camps run by the United States Justice Department for suspect Issei, immigrant Japanese, just after Pearl Harbor and to more permanent army-run camps for some of these detainees. The internment of enemy aliens during a war has a basis in law—specifically the Alien and Sedition Act of 1798—and it is governed by international accord in the form of the Geneva Conventions. The roundup and incarceration of American citizens had no legal precedent and singled out a race of people (7).
4. The article was written by John Haigh and appeared in the 6 October 1974 issue (12). The rest of the description of Evanson, including her views on the incarceration, is adapted from Haigh's article.
5. Personal communication, Seattle Retired Teachers' Association, 22 October 1996.

6. Around this time the national Redress Movement was under way and Japanese American activism was strong in Seattle and throughout the West Coast. This article may have been a response to the political situation surrounding the Redress Movement in its portrayal of a group of Nisei who felt a sense of "acceptance" at the time of their incarceration, in contrast to the activist Nisei of the 1970s.

7. John Haigh, "Children's View of the Japanese Evacuation," *Seattle Times Sunday Magazine*, 6 October 1974, 12.

8. Many sources in Asian American studies, particularly historical and literary works address this very issue.

CHAPTER 1: MAKING SENSE OF DISSONANCE

1. It was believed that some would be evacuated east of the Cascade Mountain range in Washington. This student, Tokunari, is probably referring to what was being discussed in the newspapers, on the radio, and in the community. Tokunari and his classmates were all taken first to Camp Harmony in Puyallup, Washington.

2. The style of writing of these Nisei students was also consistent and pervasive among their peers at the time. See, for example, Vincent Taijiri, *Through Innocent Eyes: Writings and Art from the Japanese American Internment by Poston I School Children* (Los Angeles: Keiro Services Press and The Generation Fund, 1990).

3. Louis Fiset, "Redress for Nisei Public Employees in Washington State after World War II, *Pacific Northwest Quarterly* 88, no.1 (winter 1996–1997): 21–32.

4. Included in the final chapter of this book.

5. Last name omitted by author.

6. Doris crossed out her original title, "Japanese Evacuation," and replaced it with "The departure" written above it.

7. Evanson's note in parentheses: "This is in Ella Evanson's handwriting—for some reason *copied* from the original of 'Ernest,' which is not in hand." No date.

8. The *Seattle Times* reported that many Nikkei were planning "farewell parties" prior to their departure to Camp Harmony in Puyallup, Washington. The specific article is "Japs, About to Go, Plan Farewells," *Seattle Times*, 26 April 1942, C1.

9. Unfortunately, the oral history narrators have no recollection of this last day at Washington School.

10. According to the Seattle Public Schools' 1927 *Triennial Report* (43), students were graded on citizenship on the basis of the following points: Courtesy, Promptness, Dependability, Cheerful Cooperation, Self-Reliance, Initiative, Thrift, Self-Control, Good Sportsmanship, School Service, and Good Workmanship.

11. Yoshiko Uchida, *The Invisible Thread* (Englewood Cliffs, N.J.: J. Messner, 1991), 69.

CHAPTER 2: SETTING THE STAGE

1. At present, the city's population is just over 540,000 (with a total of 3.1 million residing in the greater Seattle area).

2. This section on Seattle's early history is adapted from the following: Richard C. Berner's *Seattle 1900–1920: From Boomtown, Urban Turbulence, to Restoration* (Seattle: Charles Press, 1991) and *Seattle 1921–1940: From Boom to Bust* (Seattle: Charles Press, 1992). A comprehensive Internet site on Seattle's history provided a general overview of some of the topical themes I have included in this section on the history of Chinese and Japanese Americans (*www.historylink.org*).

3. U.S. Commission on Wartime Relocation and Internment of Civilians, *Personal Justice Denied* (Seattle: University of Washington Press, 1997), 28–29.

4. Ibid.

5. This section is summarized from ibid., 32–36. What I cover are the most basic laws and policies aimed against the Japanese on the West Coast.

6. Ibid., 34.

7. Yuji Ichioka, *The Issei: The World of the First Generation Japanese Immigrants, 1885–1924* (New York: The Free Press, 1988), 164–165. It is important to emphasize that the term "picture brides" is embedded in specific cultural contexts and that it should not be confused with the more denigrating form of "mail order brides" that we have at the present time. For further details on this, please see, for example, Ichioka's work cited in this note.

8. Ibid., 232.

9. Roger Daniels, *Asian America: Chinese and Japanese in the United States since 1850* (Seattle: University of Washington Press, 1988), 155.

10. Ibid.

11. S. Frank Miyamoto, "An Immigrant Community in America," in *East across the Pacific: History and Sociology Studies of Japanese Immigration and Assimilation*, ed. H. Conroy and T. S. Miyakawa, (Santa Barbara: Clio Press, 1972), 218.

12. Stephen S. Fugita and David J. O'Brien, *Japanese American Ethnicity: The Persistence of Community* (Seattle: University of Washington Press, 1991).

13. S. Frank Miyamoto, *Social Solidarity among the Japanese in Seattle*, 3rd ed. (Seattle: University of Washington Press, 1989).

14. Harry H. L. Kitano, *Generation and Identity: The Japanese Americans* (Needham Heights, Mass. Ginn Press, 1993). S. Frank Miyamoto, "Problems of Interpersonal Style among the Nisei," *Amerasia* 13 (1986–1987): 29–45.

15. George A. De Vos, "A Japanese Legacy of Confucian Thought," in *Confucianism and the Family,* ed. Walter H. Slote and George A. De Vos (Albany: State University of New York Press, 1998), 107.

16. Undoubtedly, these cultural values and norms were misunderstood to a large degree and held as extreme stereotypes that worked to label Japanese Americans as "unassimilable" and "model minorities."

17. Ichioka, *The Issei*, 196; and David A. Takami, *Divided Destiny: A History of Japanese Americans in Seattle* (Seattle: University of Washington Press, 1998), 33.

18. More details on Nisei experiences with Japanese Language Schools are revealed in chapter 6.

19. This section on Japanese Language Schools and the issue of dual citizenship is taken from Ichioka, *The Issei*, 196–205. Ichioka's account of the history and the politics of the Japanese Language Schools, including a move to ban all foreign language schools by a nativist group in California, is thoroughly addressed.

20. Ibid., 200.

21. See the following chapter for details on the Seattle Public Schools' Americanization and Citizenship Education programs.

22. Miyamoto, *Social Solidarity.* To this day, S. Frank Miyamoto's 1939 master's thesis, and the subsequent revised editions, serves as the foundational basis for documenting the early educational history of Seattle's Nisei. Current historical research on Seattle's Japanese American community all cite Miyamoto when discussing schooling prior to the evacuation. See, for example: Daniels, *Asian America*; and Yasuko Takezawa, *Breaking the Silence: Redress and Japanese American Ethnicity* (Ithaca, N.Y.: Cornell University Press, 1995). Due to the dearth of research in this area, I rely on Miyamoto's groundbreaking work in discussing early Nisei education in Seattle.

23. Bryce Nelson, *Good Schools: The Seattle Public School System, 1901–1930* (Seattle: University of Washington Press, 1988), 3–4.

24. *Histories of the Seattle Public Schools*, 1961.

25. The third group being African American.

26. *Quinquennial Report of the Board of Directors of Seattle School District No. 1* (Seattle: City of Seattle, 1921), 270–271.

27. Ibid.

28. Miyamoto, *Social Solidarity*, xv.

29. Ibid, 53.

30. Ibid, 53.

31. *Seattle Daily Times*, 25 June 1931.

32. Miyamoto, *Social Solidarity*, 53.

33. Atshushi Kiuchi. "Part of Miss Mahon's Class—Until the Internment," *Seattle Times*, 19 July 1998, Lifestyles section.

34. The written accounts in Miyamoto as well as other oral histories of Japanese Americans in Seattle indicate to varying degrees the effect of schooling in terms of Americanization. For example, Takezawa's *Breaking the Silence* offers accounts of Nisei who felt that their schooling was one of humiliation of one's home culture.

CHAPTER 3: LOOKING BACKWARD

1. *Triennial Report of the Seattle Public Schools, 1924–1927* (Seattle: Seattle Public Schools, 1927), 39.

2. Roger Sale, *Seattle, Past to Present* (Seattle: University of Washington Press, 1976).

3. A thorough account of the history of the common school movement, including a discussion of the ideological drive for many schools, can be found in Carl Kaestle's *Pillars of the Republic: Common Schools and American Society, 1780–1860* (New York: Hill and Wang, 1983).

4. An example of this can be found in Quintard Taylor's *In Search of the Racial Frontier: African Americans in the American West, 1528–1990* (New York: Norton, 1998).

5. Hawaii's Japanese American residents comprised an overwhelming 43 percent of the total population during 1920, but it was a territory and did not receive statehood until 1959. Source: Eileen Tamura, "The English-Only Effort, the

Anti-Japanese Campaign, and Language Acquisition in the Education of Japanese Americans in Hawaii, 1915–1940," *History of Education Quarterly*, no. 33 (spring 1993): 38.

6. Calvin Schmid and Wayne McVey Jr., *Growth and Distribution of Minority Races in Seattle, Washington* (Seattle: Seattle Public Schools, 1964), 14.

7. Roger Daniels, *Asian America: Chinese and Japanese in the United States since 1850* (Seattle: University of Washington Press, 1988), 156.

8. Ibid., 157.

9. Quintard Taylor, *The Forging of a Black Community: Seattle's Central District from 1870 through the Civil Rights Era* (Seattle: University of Washington Press, 1994), 118.

10. Ibid.

11. William J. Reese, *Power and Promise of School Reform: Grassroots Movements during the Progressive Era* (Boston: Routledge and Kegan Paul), 24–25.

12. Daniels, *Asian America*, 156.

13. Charlotte Brooks, "In the Twilight Zone between Black and White: Japanese American Resettlement and Community in Chicago, 1942–1945," *Journal of American History* 86, no.4 (March 2000): 1655–1687.

14. Frank B. Cooper to Mrs. Josephine Preston, state superintendent of public instruction, 18 February 1916, Seattle Public Schools' Archives and Records Management Center, Superintendent's Files.

15. Sale, *Seattle, Past to Present*, 118.

16. F .B. Cooper to J. C. Preston, 18 February 1916.

17. F. B. Cooper to J. C. Preston, 18 February 1916.

18. David Tyack and James Thomas, "Moral Majorities and the School Curriculum: Making Virtue Mandatory, 1880–1930," in Tyack and Thomas, *Law and Shaping of Public Education* (Madison: University of Wisconsin, 1987), 170–171.

19. Ibid., 171.

20. Bryce Nelson, *Good Schools: The Seattle Public School System, 1901–1930* (Seattle: University of Washington Press, 1988), 109.

21. Ibid., 111.

22. Ibid., 117.

23. *Quinquennial Report of the Board of Directors of Seattle District No. 1* (Seattle: City of Seattle, 1921), 86.

24. Winthrop Talbot, "Americanism," in *Americanization: Principles of Americanism, Essentials of Americanization, Technic of Race Assimilation, Annotated Bibliography*, ed. W. Talbot and J. A. Johnsen (New York: H. W. Wilson, 1920).

25. David Cohen, *Children of the Mill: Schooling and Society in Gary, Indiana, 1906–1960* (Bloomington: Indiana University Press, 1990), 61.

26. Council of Jewish Women, University of Washington Manuscripts and Archives Division, Accession No. 2089-29, Box 4, Folder 16.

27. *Quinquennial Report*, 87.

28. This might also have been in response to the growing number of "hyphenated" Americans in the United States and the subsequent move by some to curtail hyphenated identities.

29. Julie A. Reuben, "Beyond Politics: Community Civics and the Redefinition of Citizenship in the Progressive Era," *History of Education Quarterly* 37 (winter 1997): 399–420.

30. *Quinquennial Report*, 87.

31. *Triennial Report of the Public Schools, 1921–1924*, 16.

32. Ibid.

33. Ibid., 49.

34. Ibid., 50.

35. *Triennial Report of the Public Schools, 1924–1927* (Seattle: Seattle Public Schools, 1927), 36.

36. *Triennial Report of the Public Schools, 1921–1924*, 16.

37. *Triennial Report, 1924–1927,* 43.

38. *Triennial Report, 1921–1924,* 16.

39. Ibid., 17.

40. *Triennial Report, 1924–1927,* 36.

41. Judith Rosenberg Raftery, *Land of Fair Promise: Politics and Reform in Los Angeles Schools, 1885–1941* (Stanford: Stanford University Press, 1992), 240.

42. Ibid., 163–164.

43. *Triennial Report of the Public School, 1927–1930*, 25.

44. Ibid., 26.

45. Ibid., 27.

46. Ibid., 29.

47. Cohen, *Children of the Mill*, 23.

48. *Triennial Report, 1927–1930*, 25.

49. F. B. Cooper to the BOD, 24 September 1919, Seattle Public Schools' Archives and Records Management Center, Superintendent's Files.

50. George J. Sánchez, "'Go After the Women': Americanization and the Mexican Immigrant Women, 1915–1929," in *Unequal Sisters: A Multicultural Reader in U.S. Women's History, Second Edition*, ed. Vicki L. Ruiz and Ellen Carol Du Bois (New York: Routledge, 1994).

51. Raftery, *Land of Fair Promise*, 68.

52. Sánchez, "'Go After the Women,'" 293.

53. Council of Jewish Women, University of Washington Manuscripts and Archives Division, Accession No. 2089-29, Box 1, Folder 1.

54. Ibid.

55. *Seattle School Bulletin* 7, no. 1 (November 1919): 1.

56. *Quinquennial Report*, 87.

57. F. B. Cooper to BOD, 13 January 1922, Seattle Public Schools' Archives and Records Management Center, Superintendent's Files.

58. *Triennial Report, 1921–1924,* 74.

59. F. E. Willard to BOD, 12 March 1920, Seattle Public Schools' Archives and Records Management Center, Superintendent's Files.

60. F .B. Cooper to BOD, 13 January 1922.

61. Ibid.

62. F. B. Cooper to BOD, 20 January 1922, Seattle Public Schools' Archives and Records Management Center, Superintendent's Files.

63. Eileen Tamura, "The English-Only Effort, the Anti-Japanese Campaign, and Language Acquisition in the Education of Japanese Americans in Hawaii, 1915–1940," 38.

64. Eileen Tamura, *Americanization, Acculturation, and Ethnic Identity: The Nisei Generation in Hawaii* (Urbana: University of Illinois Press, 1994), 111.

65. Ibid.

66. Ibid.

67. Ibid., 115.

68. Personal correspondence with Eileen Tamura, 9 October 1997.

69. Nelson, *Good Schools*, 111.

70. *Triennial Report, 1921–1924*, 15.

71. *Triennial Report, 1924–1927*, 39–40.

72. Ibid., 40.

73. Ronald E. Butchart, "Punishments, Prizes, and Procedures: A History of Discipline in U.S. Schools," in *Classroom Discipline in American Schools: Problems*

and Possibilities for Democratic Education, ed., Ronald E. Butchart and Barbara McEwan (Albany: State University of New York Press, 1998), 28.

74. *Triennial Report, 1924–1927,* 42.

75. B. Edward McClellan, *Moral Education in America: Schools and the Shaping of Character from Colonial Times to the Present* (New York: Teachers College Press, Columbia University, 1999), 53.

76. Reuben, "Beyond Politics," 401.

77. Sale, *Seattle, Past to Present,* 117.

78. Seattle was founded in either November 1851 or February 1852, according to Sale, *Seattle, Past to Present,* 8.

CHAPTER 4: AMERICANIZATION BROADENED

1. I am deeply grateful to a former student of mine, Gary Davenport, for the use of one of the original copies of *Successful Living* that had been kept in his family. His grandfather, Noah Davenport, was head of the History and Social Studies Department at Franklin High School in Seattle and kept a copy of the text in his personal library. Noah Davenport is the coauthor of books on life in Seattle including *Government in Seattle: City, County, State, National,* with Samuel Fleming, assistant superintendent of schools (Seattle: Seattle Public Schools, 1935); and Living in Seattle, with Lorin Peterson, Division of Adult Education at the University of Washington and former research director of the Seattle Municipal League (Seattle: Seattle Public Schools, 1950).

2. Dominic W. Moreo, *Schools in the Great Depression* (New York: Garland, 1996), 86.

3. Ibid., 87.

4. Ibid., 86.

5. Ibid., 87.

6. Nicholas V. Montalto, *A History of the Intercultural Education Movement, 1924–1941* (New York: Garland, 1982), 126–127.

7. Stanwood Cobb, quoted in Lawrence Cremin, *The Transformation of the School: Progressivism in American Education, 1876–1957* (New York: Knopf, 1968), 241.

8. Patricia Albjerg Graham, *Progressive Education: From Arcady to Academe: A History of the Progressive Education Association 1919–1955* (New York: Teach-

ers College Press, Columbia University, 1967), 102. Graham offers one of the more comprehensive and detailed organizational and policy studies of the PEA.

9. Ronald K. Goodenow, "The Progressive Educator, Race and Ethnicity in the Depression Years: An Overview," *History of Education Quarterly* 15 (winter 1975): 374.

10. Ibid.

11. Montalto, *History of the Intercultural Education Movement*, 77. Montalto provides a thoughtful and thorough account of Rachel Davis Du Bois's professional career as the leader in intercultural education, as well as her rise and fall within the Progressive Education Association.

12. There is no relation between the two.

13. Montalto, *History of the Intercultural Education Movement*, 85.

14. Ibid., 92.

15. Rachel Davis-Du Bois, "Our Enemy—The Stereotype," *Progressive Education* 12 (March 1935): 147.

16. Ibid., 149.

17. Ibid., 147.

18. Ibid., 148.

19. *Seattle Educational Bulletin*, October 1927, 1.

20. *Seattle Educational Bulletin*, March 1934, 1.

21. *Successful Living* (Seattle: Seattle Public Schools, 1935), 1.

22. *Successful Living*, 3.

23. Ibid., 4.

24. Ibid.

25. Ibid., 11.

26. Ibid., 46.

27. *Living Today—Learning for Tomorrow* (Seattle: Seattle Public Schools, 1938), 12–14.

28. Ibid., 16.

29. Ibid.

30. Ibid.

31. Ibid., 17.

32. Ibid., 18.

33. Ibid., 73.

34. Ibid., 82.

35. *Successful Living*, 15–16.

36. Ibid., 6.

37. Vanessa Siddle Walker, *Their Highest Potential: An African American School Community in the Segregated South* (Chapel Hill: University of North Carolina Press, 1996), 125.

38. *Successful Living*, 19.

39. The chapter on "Individual Guideposts" in *Successful Living* gives an example of a student's overcoming his prejudice toward his own race. The section, titled "I Belong to an Inferior Race," is as follows: "Dick was overheard to say, 'I have no chance. I belong to an inferior race.' A few days later, through pictures, poems, and stories, he was surprised to find that his race possessed outstanding qualities and characteristics. There was a marked change in his attitude which not only changed his type of school work, but also carried over into the home" (*Successful Living*, 157). Such examples of highpoints in classroom activities concentrated on students' prejudiced beliefs and attitudes toward different (or of their own) races or cultures, and how subsequent teachings helped to overcome stereotypes.

40. Walker, *Their Highest Potential*, 109.

41. Ibid., 109–110.

42. Ibid., 111.

43. *Montalto, History of the Intercultural Education Movement*, 85.

44. Ibid., 90.

45. Ibid., 91.

46. *Successful Living*, 46.

47. Ibid., 59.

48. Ibid.

49. Ibid., 46.

CHAPTER 5: TENUOUS CITIZENSHIP

1. *Seattle Schools* 18, no. 5 (January 1942): 1. Cambell was assistant superintendent and a member of the Seattle Municipal Defense Commission.

2. *Seattle Exchange*, May 1942, 7. Over the years there were inconsistencies in the title (*Seattle Principals' Exchange* and *Seattle Principal's Exchange*) of this publication. My placement of the apostrophe in this and subsequent entries reflect such changes over time.

3. *Seattle Educational Bulletin*, November 1937, 1.

4. *Histories of the Seattle Public Schools* (Seattle: Seattle Public Schools, 1961).

5. Petronilla Fitzgerald taught art at Washington School as indicated in the *1941–1942 Seattle Public Schools' Directory.*

6. See, for example: Thomas F. Gossett's *Race: The History of an Idea in America* (New York: Oxford University Press, 1997); Stephen J. Gould's *The Mismeasure of Man* (New York: Norton, 1996); Michael Omi and Howard Winant's *Racial Formation in the United States: From the 1960s to the 1990s* (New York: Routledge, 1994); Steven Selden's *Inheriting Shame: The Story of Eugenics and Racism in America* (New York: Teachers College Press, Columbia University, 1999); and Ronald Takaki's *Iron Cages: Race and Culture in 19th-Century America, Revised Edition* (New York: Oxford University Press, 2000).

7. "Minutes of the Business and Professional Women's Evening Committee of the Seattle Council of Jewish Women," 17 April 1939, Council of Jewish Women, University of Washington Manuscripts and Archives Division, Accession No. 2089-29, Box 6, Folder 25.

8. Washington School had a mixture of students from different backgrounds. Because I could not discern the ethnicities of students in this section, I refer to them as "non-Nisei," that is, they were most likely European American, Jewish, and African American students.

9. David A. Takami, *Divided Destiny: A History of Japanese Americans in Seattle* (Seattle University of Washington Press, 1998), 41.

10. "736 Japanese Arrested in U.S. and Hawaii," *Seattle Times*, 8 December 1941, 1.

11. Takami, *Divided Destiny*, 42.

12. "War Orders Stop Japanese Travel," *Seattle Times*, 8 December 1941, 2.

13. "Total Curb on Japanese Funds," *Seattle Times*, 8 December 1941, 22.

14. "Nippon School Here Is Closed," *Seattle Times*, 9 December 1941, 2.

15. Ibid.

16. "American-Born Japanese Loyal, Editor Asserts," *Seattle Times*, 8 December 1941, 2.

17. "1,300 Seattle Japanese Pledge Loyalty," *Seattle Times*, 23 December 1941, 8.

18. "Churchmen Ask Friendship for Japanese Here," *Seattle Times*, 10 December 1941, 10.

19. "200 More Japs Seized by F.B.I. In California," *Seattle Times*, 19 February 1942, 8. "23 Japanese Seized in Portland Raids," *Seattle Times*, 19 February 1942, 8.

20. "Danger of Jap Attack on Coast 'Heightened'" *Seattle Times*, 1 February 1942, C1.

21. "Korean Urges Interning of All Japanese," *Seattle Times*, 19 February 1942, 8. The history of Japanese colonization in Korea coupled with Korean Americans'

heightened sense of nationalism for their home country—as they were displaced nationals, subject to Japanese rule in Korea—was one reason for their public support of the evacuation. Another reason, much like the case of Chinese Americans, lay in their fear that mainstream Americans would not be able to tell them apart from Japanese Americans, thus resulting in potential acts of violence and further discrimination. "Move Japs, Say 4 More Posts," in *Seattle Times*, 19 February 1942, 11. "Portland Council Urges Moving All Japanese," *Seattle Times*, 20 February 1942, 13.

22. Hisa Kato, in her oral history in chapter 6, discusses the influence of the Good American Citizens' Club during her time as a student at Bailey Gatzert.

23. "320 Bailey Gatzert Jap Pupils Face Unfinished School Term." in *Seattle Times,* 23 March 1942, 2.

24. Ibid.

25. "Nisei Reaffirm Loyalty to U.S.," *Seattle Times*, 20 February 1942, 16.

26. "Japanese Are Ready to Obey Moving Order," *Seattle Times*, 24 February 1942, 4.

27. Takami, *Divided Destiny*, 48

CHAPTER 6: DISSONANCE EMBODIED

1. I, however, did not limit their recollections to just that period in their lives. The sum of their life experiences necessarily includes their evacuation to Puyallup and then to Hunt, Idaho (also referred to by the narrators and fellow Nisei as Minidoka Camp, Idaho).

2. Valerie Yow, *Recording Oral History: A Practical Guide for Social Scientists* (Thousand Oaks, Calif.: Sage, 1994), 14.

3. Ibid., 15.

4. See for example: William Dean Zeller, *The Educational Program Provided the Japanese Americans during the Relocation Period 1942–1945* (East Lansing: Michigan State University, 1963). Zeller's research provides a thorough account of the types of democratic citizenship education provided in the camps by Stanford University's Graduate School of Education Summer Course headed by Professor Paul Hanna in 1942. Thomas James's *Exile Within: The Schooling of Japanese Americans 1942–1945* (Cambridge, Mass: Harvard University Press, 1987) also describes the incongruity between democratic values as taught and life as experienced in the camps.

5. Hisako Kato, 18 May 1998, Interview by author, Seattle.

6. Matsubara is Hisa's maiden name.

7. The characterizations of the oral history narrators should be placed within the general context of the redress movement that began in the 1970s, culminating in the passage of the Civil Liberties Act of 1988. Some Nikkei who were formerly bitter and angry found the movement to be a cathartic experience as they provided testimony to the Commission on Wartime Relocation and Internment of Civilians, with many more following suit. Thus the level of reflection and analysis provided by the narrators today was aided by the activism of Nisei and Sansei during the redress movement. Also see Leslie T. Hatamiya, *Righting a wrong: Japanese Americans and the Passage of the Civil Liberties Act of 1988* (Stanford: Stanford University Press, 1993).

8. Monica Sone, *Nisei Daughter* (Seattle: University of Washington Press, 1985), 4.

9. Eileen Tamura, *Americanization, Acculturation, and Ethnic Identity: The Nisei Generation in Hawaii* (Urbana: University of Illinois Press), provides oral history accounts of Nisei experiences in Japanese Language Schools in Hawaii.

10. S. Frank Miyamoto, *Social Solidarity among the Japanese in Seattle* (Seattle: University of Washington Press, 1989), 53.

11. The history of Seattle's Central District can be found in Quintard Taylor, *The Forging of a Black Community: Seattle's Central District from 1870 through the Civil Rights Era* (Seattle: University of Washington Press, 1994).

12. Associated Press, "Japanese Attacked on New York Street: Beaten Nipponese Escapes in Hallway," *Los Angeles Times*, 9 December 1941, 16. Other news of violent outbreaks against Nikkei, in Seattle and elsewhere, are reported in the following: "Japanese Says He Was Beaten," *Seattle Times*, 11 December 1941, 20. "Stockton Japanese Killed by Filipino," *Seattle Times*, 26 December 1941, 26. "Man Admits He Shot Japanese," *Seattle Times*, 11 January 1942, 5.

13. There were four cases that were appealed to the U.S. Supreme Court during World War II. Gordon Hirabayashi and Minoru Yasui challenged the unlawful curfew. Fred Korematsu challenged the exclusion order. The only successfully appealed case was that of Mitsuye Endo, challenging the legality of the incarceration itself through a habeas corpus proceeding. For more on this, refer to Roger Daniels et al., eds., *Japanese Americans: From Relocation to Redress* (Seattle: University of Washington Press, 1994); and Peter Irons, *Justice at War: The Story of the Japanese American Internment Cases* (Berkeley: University of California Press, 1983).

14. Mitsie Fujii, 19 May 1998, Interview by author, Seattle.

15. Mitsie's maiden name is Ideta.

16. That is all the information Mitsie has on her father's arrival in the United States. She wishes she had taken the time to document his life as she felt he led a very interesting and unusual existence, "atypical" of many Issei at the time.

17. While the exact conditions in which the Idetas moved to Des Moines, Iowa, are unknown, there are cases of over 5,500 Nisei who left the concentration camps to attend college outside the West Coast exclusion zone (typically in the Midwest), aided by the National Japanese American Student Relocation Council—founded in 1942 by concerned educators who sought to provide continued education for college Nisei. A more detailed account of this can be found in Gary Okihiro's *Storied Lives: Japanese American Students and World War II* (Seattle: University of Washington Press, 1999) and Valerie Matsumoto's "Japanese American Women during World War II," in *Unequal Sisters: A Multicultural Reader in U. S. Women's History, Second Edition,* ed. Vicki L. Ruiz and Ellen Carol Du Bois, (New York: Routledge, 1994), 436–449. Additional examples can be found in Thomas James's *Exile Within* and Robert W. O'Brien's *The College Nisei* (New York: Reprinted by Arno Press, [1949] 1979).

18. Martha C. Mortensen wrote about Washington School and the moral leadership provided by Principal Sears in an article titled "War and the Children," which appeared in the *Seattle Principal's Exchange*, May 1942.

19. Kaz Ishimitsu, 10 June 1998, Interview by author, Bellevue, Wash.

20. According to Atshushi Kiuchi, in a 1998 article he wrote for the *Seattle Times*, Mahon was Irish.

21. Kaz Ishimitsu is most likely referring to the quiet meditation offered in the homerooms as described in *Successful Living* (11).

22. Also the title of Bill Hosokawa's book on the incarceration experience of Nisei, *Nisei: The Quiet Americans: The Story of a People* (Niwot: University Press of Colorado, 1992).

23. The 442nd was widely known for the all-Nisei unit, which was one of the most decorated that served during World War II. Their proof of loyalty and citizenship in this regard was still held suspect by the likes of General DeWitt. For an extensive look at this contribution by Nisei veterans, see, for example, U.S. Commission on War time Relocation and Internment of Civilians, *Personal Justice Denied* (Seattle: University of Washington Press, 1997): Carina A. Del Rosario's *A Different Battle: Stories of Asian Pacific American Veterans* (Seattle: Wing Luke Asian Museum, 1999): and Chester Tanaka's *Go for Broke: A Pictor-*

ial History of the Japanese American 100th Infantry Battalion and the 442nd Regimental Combat Team (Novato, Calif.: Presidio Press, 1982).

24. This idea is very much reflected in a 30 March 1942 issue of *Life* in its Pictures to the Editor section. A series of photographs depicts what the "average American boy," who happens to be blonde and Caucasian, does as part of his daily routines. The photos show the boy doing homework, practicing violin, receiving a toy rifle from his father, and lastly pointing his rifle at a caricature of the "Enemy Alien" Japanese as his sister points amusingly at the sketch. The message, that part of what every "American" child is supposed to do is hate the Japanese, was very clear.

25. Sample letters were given to the narrators in which to respond. Hisa's reference to the first letter has to do with the first sample letter given to her.

CONCLUSION

1. *Personal Justice Denied* (Seattle: University of Washington Press, 1997), 459.
2. That does not mean, however, that racism and discrimination did not always exist at some level.
3. In terms of current multicultural education and approaches to caring, see, for example, Valerie Ooka Pang's *Multicultural Education: A Caring-Centered, Reflective Approach* (New York: McGraw-Hill, 2001).
4. Walt Crowley, *Rites of Passage: A Memoir of the Sixties in Seattle* (Seattle: University of Washington Press, 1995), 260

A NOTE ON METHOD AND SOURCES

1. See for example: James D. Anderson, *The Education of Blacks in the South, 1860–1935* (Chapel Hill: University of North Carolina Press, 1998). Ronald D. Cohen, *Children of the Mill: Schooling and Society in Gary, Indiana, 1906–1960* (Bloomington: Indiana University Press, 1990). William J. Reese, *Power and Promise of School Reform: Grassroots Movements during the Progressive Era* (Boston: Routledge and Kegan Paul, 1988). David Tyack, Robert Lowe, and Elizabeth Hansot, eds., *Public Schools in Hard Times: The Great Depression and Recent Years* (Cambridge, Mass.: Harvard University Press, 1984). Vanessa Siddle Walker, *Their Highest Potential: An African American School Community in*

the Segregated South (Chapel Hill: University of North Carolina Press, 1996). David Adams, *Education for Extinction: American Indians and the Boarding School Experience, 1875–1928* (Lawrence: University of Kansas Press, 1995). George Sánchez, *Becoming Mexican American: Ethnicity, Culture and Identity in Chicano Los Angeles, 1900–1945* (New York: Oxford University Press, 1993).

2. Dominic W. Moreo, *Schools in the Great Depression* (New York: Garland, 1996). Bryce Nelson, *Good Schools: The Seattle Public School System, 1901–1930* (Seattle: University of Washington Press, 1988).

3. Judith Rosenberg Raftery, *Land of Fair Promise: Politics and Reform in Los Angeles Schools, 1885–1941* (Stanford: Stanford University Press, 1992).

4. Eileen Tamura, *Americanization, Acculturation, and Ethnic Identity* (Urbana: University of Illinois Press, 1994).

5. S. Frank Miyamoto, *Social Solidarity among the Japanese in Seattle* (Seattle: University of Washington, 1939).

6. Michi Nishiura Weglyn, *Years of Infamy: The Untold Story of America's Concentration Camps* (Seattle: University of Washington Press, 1976, 1996). This provides a thorough documented account from archival records. Weglyn was the first former internee to write a historical account of the experience.

7. Roger Daniels, Sandra C. Taylor, and Harry H.L. Kitano, eds., *Japanese Americans: From Relocation to Redress, Revised Edition* (Seattle: University of Washington Press, 1994).

8. Roger Daniels, *Prisoners without Trial: Japanese Americans in World War II* (New York: Hill and Wang, 1993).

9. Gary Okihiro, *Whispered Silences: Japanese Americans and World War II* (Seattle: University of Washington Press, 1996).

10. The Commission on Wartime Relocation and Internment of Civilians, *Personal Justice Denied* (Seattle: University of Washington Press, 1997).

11. Arthur A. Hansen and Betty E. Miston, eds., *Voices Long Silent: An Oral Inquiry into the Japanese American Evacuation* (Fullerton: Japanese American Project, California State University, Fullerton Oral History Program, 1974).

12. John Tateishi, *And Justice for All: An Oral History of the Japanese American Detention Camps* (New York: Random House, 1984).

13. *Densho: The Japanese American Legacy Project* (Seattle: The Densho Project, 2000). This is a digitized archive of oral histories based in Seattle, Washington. More information can be accessed at *http://www.densho.org/*

14. Robert O'Brien, *College Nisei* (Palo Alto: Pacific Books, 1949).

15. Bill Hosokawa, *Nisei: The Quiet Americans: The Story of a People* (Niwot: University Press of Colorado, 1992).

16. Yuji Ichioka, *The Issei: The World of the First Generation Japanese Immigrants, 1885–1924* (New York: Free Press, 1988).

17. Kazuo Ito, *Issei : A History of Japanese Immigrants in North America,* trans. Shinichiro Nakamura and Jean S. Gerard (Seattle: Japanese Community Service, 1973).

18. James Watanabe, *History of the Japanese of Tacoma,* trans. from the Japanese by James Watanabe (Seattle: Pacific Northwest District Council, Japanese American Citizen League, 1988).

19. Linda Tamura, *The Hood River Issei: An Oral History of Japanese Settlers in Oregon's Hood River Valley* (Urbana: University of Illinois Press, 1993).

20. Thomas Heuterman, *The Burning Horse: The Japanese-American Experience in the Yakima Valley, 1920–1942* (Cheney: Eastern Washington University Press, 1995).

21. Walter Parker, *Educating the Democratic Mind* (Albany: State University of New York Press, 1996).

22. John Dewey, *Democracy and Education* (New York: Free Press, 1944), 87.

23. *Successful Living* (Seattle: Seattle Public Schools, 1935), 4.

24. *Histories of the Seattle Public Schools* (Seattle: Seattle Public Schools, 1961).

25. "New Instructional Practices," *Seattle Principal's Exchange* 15, no.2 (November 1940), 2. Seattle Public Schools' Archives and Records Management Center.

26. Thomas Bender, "Wholes and Parts: The Need for Synthesis in American History," *Journal of American History* 73 (1986): 130–131.

APPENDIX

1. The chronology is taken from the following source: Roger Daniels et al eds., *Japanese Americans: From Relocation to Redress* (Seattle: University of Washington Press, 1994).

BIBLIOGRAPHY

★ ★ ★ ★ ★

ARCHIVAL SOURCES AND COLLECTIONS

Council of Jewish Women. University of Washington Manuscripts and Archives, Accession No. 2089-29.

Ella Evanson Papers. University of Washington Manuscripts and Archives, Accession No. 2402.

E. B. Willis Papers. University of Washington Manuscripts and Archives, Accession No. 2583–6, Box 1.

Seattle Public Schools' Archives and Records Management Center, Superintendent's Files, 1914–1953, Accession No. E427-E428, Boxes 1 and 2.

Seattle Public Schools' Archives and Records Management Center's General Collections:

Living Today—Learning for Tomorrow. Seattle: Seattle Public Schools, 1938.

Quinquennial Report of the Board of Directors of Seattle School District No. 1. Seattle: City of Seattle, 1921.

Seattle Educational Bulletin. Seattle: Seattle Public Schools, January 1925–June 1942.

Seattle Principal's Exchange. Seattle: Seattle Public Schools, February 1941 and May 1942.

*Seattle School Bulletin.*Seattle: Seattle Public Schools, November 1919.

Seattle Schools. Seattle: Seattle Public Schools, January 1942.

Successful Living. Seattle: Seattle Public Schools:, 1935.

Triennial Report of the Public Schools, 1921–1924. Seattle: Seattle Public Schools, 1924.

Triennial Report of the Public Schools, 1924—1927. Seattle: Seattle Public Schools, 1927.

NEWSPAPERS AND PERIODICALS

Life, 8 December, 1941– 1 May, 1942

Seattle Times, 8 December, 1941–1 May, 1942

Time, 8 December, 1941–1 May, 1942

ORAL HISTORY INTERVIEWS

Kato, Hisako. 18 May 1998. Interview by author, Seattle.

Fujii, Mitsie. 19 May 1998. Interview by author, Seattle.

Ishimitsu, Kazuo. 10 June 1998. Interview by author, Bellevue, Wash.

SECONDARY SOURCES

Adams, David. 1995. *Education for Extinction: American Indians and the Boarding School Experience, 1875–1928*. Lawrence: University of Kansas Press.

Anderson, James D. 1988. *The Education of Blacks in the South, 1860–1935*. Chapel Hill: University of North Carolina Press.

Bender, Thomas. 1986. "Wholes and Parts: The Need for Synthesis in American History." *Journal of American History* 73: 120–136.

Berner, Richard C. 1991. *Seattle 1900–1920: From Boomtown, Urban Turbulence, to Restoration*. Seattle: Charles Press.

———. *Seattle 1921–1940: From Boom to Bust*. Seattle: Charles Press.

Brooks, Charlotte. 2000. "In the Twilight Zone between Black and White: Japanese American Resettlement and Community in Chicago, 1942–1945." *Journal of American History* 86 (4): 1655–1687.

Bulosan, Carlos. [1943] 1996. *America Is in the Heart*. Seattle: University of Washington Press.

Burke, Edward, and Elizabeth Burke. 1979. *Seattle's Other History: Our Asian-American Heritage*. Seattle: Profanity Hill Press.

Butchart, Ronald E. 1998. "Punishments, Prizes, and Procedures: A History of Disciplines in U.S. Schools." In *Classroom Discipline in American Schools: Problems and Possibilities for Democratic Education*. Edited by Ronald E. Butchart and Barbara McEwan. Albany: State University of New York Press.

Carnes, Jim. 1995. *Us and Them: A History of Intolerance in America*. Montgomery, Ala.: Teaching Tolerance.

Chan, Sucheng. 1991. *Asian Americans: An Interpretive History*. New York: Twayne.

Cohen, Ronald D. 1990. *Children of the Mill: Schooling and Society in Gary, Indiana, 1906–1960*. Bloomington: Indiana University Press.

Cohen, Ronald D., and Raymond A. Mohl. 1979. *The Paradox of Progressive Education: The Gary Plan*. Port Washington, N.Y.: Kennikat Press.

Cremin, Lawrence. 1968. *The Transformation of the School: Progressivism in American Education, 1876–1957*. New York: Knopf.

Crowley, Walt. 1995. *Rites of Passage: A Memoir of the Sixties in Seattle*. Seattle: University of Washington Press.

Daniels, Roger. 1988. *Asian America: Chinese and Japanese in the United States since 1850*. Seattle: University of Washington Press.

———. 1993. *Prisoners without Trial: Japanese Americans in World War II*. New York: Hill and Wang.

———. 1997. "The Exile and Return of Seattle's Japanese." *Pacific Northwest Quarterly* 88 (4): 166–173.

Daniels, Roger, Sandra C. Taylor, and Harry H. L. Kitano, eds. 1994. *Japanese Americans: From Relocation to Redress*. Rev. ed. Seattle: University of Washington Press.

Davis-Du Bois, Rachel. 1935. "Our Enemy—The Stereotype." *Progressive Education* 12 (3): 146–150.

Del Rosario, Carina A. 1999. *A Different Battle: Stories of Asian Pacific American Veterans*. Seattle: Wing Luke Museum.

Dewey, John. 1944. *Democracy and Education*. New York: Free Press.

Fiset, Louis. 1996–1997. "Redress for Nisei Public Employees in Washington State after World War II." *Pacific Northwest Quarterly* 88 (1): 21–32.

Fugita, Stephen S., and David J. O'Brien. 1991. *Japanese American Ethnicity: The Persistence of Community*. Seattle: University of Washington Press.

Goodenow, Ronald K. 1975. "The Progressive Educator, Race and Ethnicity in the Depression Years: An Overview." *History of Education Quarterly* 15 (4): 365–394.

Gossett, Thomas F. 1997. *Race: The History of an Idea in America*. New ed. New York: Oxford University Press.

Gould, Stephen J. 1996. *The Mismeasure of Man*. New York: Norton.

Graham, Patricia Albjerg. 1967. *Progressive Education: From Arcady to Academe: A History of the Progressive Education Association 1919–1955*. New York: Teachers College Press, Columbia University.

Greenberg, Cheryl. 1995. "Black and Jewish Response to Japanese Internment." *Journal of American Ethnic History* 14 (2): 3–37.

Gulick, Sidney L. 1920. "Are Japanese Assimilable?" In *Americanization: Principals of Americanism, Essentials of Americanization, Technic of Race-Assimilation, Annotated Bibliography*. Edited by W. Talbot and J. E. Johnsen. New York: H. W. Wilson.

Haigh, John. 1974. "Children's View of the Japanese Evacuation." *Seattle Times Sunday Magazine*, 6 October, 12.

Hansen, Arthur A., ed. 1991. *Japanese American World War II Evacuation Oral History Project, Part I: Internees*. Westport, Conn.: Meckler.

Hatamiya, Leslie T. 1993. *Righting a Wrong: Japanese Americans and the Passage of the Civil Liberties Act of 1988*. Stanford: Stanford University Press.

Helmreich, William. 1982. *The Things They Say behind Your Back*. Garden City, N.Y.: Doubleday.

Heuterman, Thomas. 1995. *The Burning Horse: The Japanese-American Experience in the Yakima Valley, 1920–1942*. Cheney: Eastern Washington University Press.

Hosokawa, Bill. 1992. *Nisei: The Quiet Americans: The Story of a People*. Niwot: University Press of Colorado.

Ichioka, Yuji. 1988. *The Issei: The World of the First Generation Japanese Immigrants, 1885–1924*. New York: Free Press.

Irons, Peter. 1983. *Justice at War: The Story of the Japanese American Internment Cases*. Berkeley: University of California Press.

Ito, Kazuo. 1973. *Issei: A History of Japanese Immigrants in North America*. Translated by Shinichiro Nakamura and Jean S. Gerard. Seattle: Japanese Community Service.

James, Thomas. 1987. *Exile Within: The Schooling of Japanese Americans 1942–1945*. Cambridge, Mass.: Harvard University Press.

Kitano, Harry H. L. 1993. *Generation and Identity: The Japanese Americans*. Needham Heights, Mass.: Ginn Press.

Kitano, Harry H. L., and Roger Daniels. 1988. *Asian Americans: Emerging Minorities.* Englewood Cliffs, N.J.: Prentice Hall.

Kiuchi, Atshushi. 1998. "Part of Miss Mahon's Class—Until the Internment." *Seattle Times,* July 19, Lifestyles section.

Matsumoto, Valerie. 1994. "Japanese American Women during World War II." In *Unequal Sisters: A Multicultural Reader in U.S. Women's History, Second Edition.* Edited by Vicki Ruiz and Ellen Carol Du Bois. New York: Routledge.

McClellan, B. Edward. 1999. *Moral Education in America: Schools and the Shaping of Character from Colonial Times to the Present.* New York: Teachers College Press, Columbia University.

Miyamoto, S. Frank. 1939. *Social Solidarity among the Japanese in Seattle.* 3d Ed., 1989 ed. Seattle: University of Washington Press.

———. 1972. "An Immigrant Community in America." In *East across the Pacific: Historical and Sociology Studies of Japanese Immigration and Assimiliation.* Edited by H. Conroy and T. S. Miyakawa. Santa Barbara: Clio Press.

———. 1986–1987."Problems of Interpersonal Style among the Nisei." *Amerasia* 13 (2): 29–45.

Montalto, Nicholas V. 1982. *A History of the Intercultural Educational Movement, 1924–1941.* New York: Garland.

Moreo, Dominic W. 1996. *Schools in the Great Depression.* New York: Garland.

Mullins, Joseph G. 1978. *Hawaiian Journey.* Honolulu: Mutual.

Nelson, Bryce. 1988. *Good Schools: The Seattle Public School System, 1901–1930.* Seattle: University of Washington Press.

O'Brien, Robert. [1949] 1979 *The College Nisei.* New York: Reprinted by Arno Press.

Okihiro, Gary. 1996. *Whispered Silences: Japanese Americans and World War II.* Seattle: University of Washington Press.

———. 1999. *Storied Lives: Japanese American Students and World War II.* Seattle: University of Washington Press.

Omi, Michael, and Howard Winant. 1994. *Racial Formation in the United States: From the 1960s to the 1990s.* 2d ed. New York: Routledge.

Pang, Valerie Ooka. 2001. *Multicultural Education: A Caring-Centered Reflective Approach.* New York: McGraw-Hill.

Parker, Walter C., ed. 1996. *Educating the Democratic Mind.* Albany: State University of New York Press.

Raftery, Judith Rosenberg. 1992. *Land of Fair Promise: Politics and Reform in Los Angeles Schools, 1885–1941.* Stanford: Stanford University Press.

Reese, William J. 1988. *Power and Promise of School Reform: Grassroots Movements during the Progressive Era*. Boston: Routledge and Kegan Paul.

Reuben, Julie A. 1997. "Beyond Politics: Community Civics and the Redefinition of Citizenship in the Progressive Era." *History of Education Quarterly* 37 (4): 399–420.

Roosevelt, Theodore. 1920. "Fear God and Take Your Own Part (1915)." In *Americanization: Principles of Americanism, Essentials of Americanization, Technic of Race Assimilation, Annotated Bibliography*. Edited by W. Talbot and J. A. Johnsen. New York: H. W. Wilson.

Sale, Roger. 1976. *Seattle, Past to Present*. Seattle: University of Washington Press.

Sánchez, George J. 1993. *Becoming Mexican American: Ethnicity, Culture and Identity in Chicano Los Angeles, 1900–1945*. New York: Oxford University Press.

Sánchez, George J. "'Go After the Women': Americanization and Mexican Immigrant Women, 1915–1929." In *Unequal Sisters: A Multicultural Reader in the U.S. Women's History, Second Edition*. Edited by Vicki Ruiz and Ellen Carol Du Bois. New York: Routledge.

Schmid, Calvin F., and Wayne McVey Jr. 1964. *Growth and Distribution of Minority Races in Seattle*. Seattle: Seattle Public Schools.

Sone, Monica. 1985. *Nisei Daughter*. Seattle: University of Washington Press.

Taijiri, Vincent, ed. 1990. *Through Innocent Eyes: Writings and Art from the Japanese American Internment by Poston I School Children*. Los Angeles: Keiro Services Press and The Generation Fund.

Takaki, Ronald. 1989. *Strangers from a Different Shore*. New York: Penguin Books.

———. 1990. *Iron Cages: Race and Culture in 19th-Century America*. New York: Oxford University Press.

———. 1993. *A Different Mirror*. Boston: Back Bay.

Takami, David A. 1998. *Divided Destiny: A History of Japanese Americans in Seattle*. Seattle: University of Washington Press.

Takezawa, Yasuko. 1995. *Breaking the Silence: Redress and Japanese American Ethnicity*. Ithaca, N.Y.: Cornell University Press.

Talbot, Winthrop. 1920. "Americanism." In *Americanization: Principles of Americanism, Essentials of Americanization, Technic of Race Assimilation, Annotated Bibliography*. Edited by W. Talbot and J. A. Johnsen. New York: H. W. Wilson.

Tamura, Eileen. 1993. "The English-Only Effort, the Anti-Japanese Campaign, and Language Acquisition in the Education of Japanese Americans in Hawaii,

1915–40." *History of Education Quarterly* (no. 33): 37–57.

———. 1994. *Americanization, Acculturation, and Ethnic Identity: The Nisei Generation in Hawaii*. Urbana: University of Illinois Press.

Tamura, Linda. 1993. *The Hood River Issei: An Oral History of Japanese Settlers in Oregon's Hood River Valley*. Urbana: University of Illinois Press.

Tanaka, Chester. 1982. *Go for Broke: A Pictorial History of the Japanese American 100th Infantry Battalion and the 442nd Regimental Combat Team*. Navato, CA: Presidio Press.

Tateishi, John. 1984. *And Justice For All: An Oral History of the Japanese American Detention Camps*. New York: Random House.

Taylor, Quintard. 1994. *The Forging of a Black Community: Seattle's Central District from 1870 through the Civil Rights Era*. Seattle: University of Washington Press.

———. 1998. *In Search of the Racial Frontier: African Americans in the American West, 1528–1990*. New York: Norton.

Tyack, David, Robert Lowe, and Elizabeth Hansot. 1984. *Public Schools in Hard Times: The Great Depression and Recent Years*. Cambridge, Mass.: Harvard University Press.

Tyack, David, and James Thomas. 1987. "Moral Majorities and the School Curriculum: Making Virtue Mandatory, 1880–1930." In *Law and Shaping of Public Education*. Edited by D. Tyack and J. Thomas. Madison: University of Wisconsin.

Uchida, Yoshiko. 1991. *The Invisible Thread*. Englewood Cliffs, N.J.: Messner.

United States Commission on Wartime Relocation and Internment of Civilians. 1997. *Personal Justice Denied*. Seattle: University of Washington Press.

Walker, Vanessa Siddle. 1996. *Their Highest Potential: An African American School Community in the Segregated South*. Chapel Hill, University of North Carolina Press.

Watanabe, James. 1988. *History of the Japanese of Tacoma*. Translated from the Japanese by James Watanabe. Seattle: Pacific Northwest District Council, Japanese American Citizen League.

Weglyn, Michi Nishiura. [1976] 1996. *Years of Infamy: The Untold Story of Americas Concentration Camps*. Seattle: University of Washington Press.

White, Richard. 1998. *Remembering Ahanagran: Storytelling in a Family's Past*. New York: Hill and Wang.

Yow, Valerie. 1994. *Recording Oral History: A Practical Guide for Social Scientists*. Thousand Oaks, Calif.: Sage.

Zeller, William Dean. 1963. *The Educational Program Provided the Japanese Americans during Relocation Period 1942–1945*. East Lansing: Michigan State University Press.

INDEX

★ ★ ★ ★ ★